M000168091

DISTILLED

DISTILLED

From absinthe & brandy to gin & whisky,
the world's finest spirits unearthed, explained & enjoyed

Joel Harrison & Neil Ridley

MITCHELL BEAZLEY

CONTENTS

INTRODUCTION

Welcome to Distilled

Throughout this book, we aim to act as your Sherpa up the mountain of distilled drinks, your captain on the vodka voyager, your buddy on brandy; we offer to be your guide on the cocktail trail and your supplier of wisdom on whisky. However, this is not a complete tome of information, an almanac of Armagnacs, a textbook on Tequila. This is our guide to exploring some of the greatest spirits on the market today, which you may not have heard of or tasted before, but should certainly seek out to the best of your abilities.

Think of this as a city guide; we will take you by the hand and lead you to the boutiques and the artisanal coffee shops and bakeries. But we will also look at the more intriguing offerings from some of the established producers. With the growth of creativity in the spirits world and small producers starting up across the globe, the bigger players have to compete by developing new products, and we are here to throw the spotlight on these supporting artists, away from the main headline acts. You may one day see these brands or products on the main stage, but for now they are very much on the fringe.

For both of us, the journey into the world of spirits has been a truly enlightening experience, and in uncovering the gems we have listed in the various "10 to Try" sections, we are offering you our impressions of the most interesting examples out there rather than specifically "the best". Not only that, but within each spirit chapter you will find a "Meet the Maverick" section, where we have sought out some of the most colourful characters either making or working with spirits today to tell it like it is, and whose stories are so engaging that you will also want to share a drink or two with them. And when it actually comes to drinking these fine spirits... well, we'll give you as many pointers as we can to ensure you are getting as much enjoyment from them as we are: from the finest must-try cocktails to the simple techniques, rituals, and serves that these little beauties all fully deserve.

HOW
DISTILLED
WORKS

To summarize the characteristics of every spirit across the globe in one handy drinker's guide is quite a challenge, so in short we have focused on the main spirit types that you will find in the back bar of most well-stocked and versatile outlets. Within each spirit chapter, we profile, where appropriate, a few other suggested spirits that share a similar production method or flavour profile as the main one.

We have prepared a list of key facts (Our Spirit "Thumbnails") for each spirit to give you the very basics of what to expect.

OUR SPIRIT
"THUMBNAILS"

SPIRIT NAME	ETYMOLOGY/ COUNTRY OF ORIGIN	COLOUR	MAIN COUNTRIES OF PRODUCTION	BIGGEST SELLING GLOBAL BRANDS	KEY INGREDIENTS
Some spirits have the same name but with slightly different spellings. We aim to explain where these are derived from historically.	Everything has to start somewhere, so consider this your first port of call. Some spirits, such as brandy and whisky, have various locations that claim their provenance, so let battle commence!	This is purely a guideline on the sort of thing to look for. Of course, every spirit has its own particular shade or idiosyncrasy to consider, especially those that are matured or aged in wood.	This will tell you the hotspots for the spirit today, from mass-produced, mass-marketed mega brands through to small, hand-bottled batches.	We would be foolish not to tell you who's doing well, wouldn't we? Here, it's worth remembering that, while these are HUGE brands, one shouldn't always write them off just because they are popular.	This was historically defined by what grew well in a particular location. Today, the landscape has changed, and, from grape to grain and potato to plum, the type of base ingredient will have a huge influence on the outcome of a particular spirit, from both a flavour and an economic point of view.

You may not agree with all of our choices and you may have other suggestions for spirits that are just too exquisite to ignore. But that's the beauty of opinion, and in reading this book we hope you are inspired to take a spirited voyage for yourself, perhaps bringing along a more-than-willing crew of able shipmates too.

As our good friend, master blender and fellow spirits explorer John Glaser from the wonderful specialist Scotch whisky company Compass Box, says, "Above all, share and enjoy!"

Joel Harrison and Neil Ridley

A POTTED HISTORY OF

Potables

Like all great stories, the history of distillation is mysterious, engaging, and ambiguous, with different nations each adding their own inimitable stamp on traditional techniques that are still practised today in virtually every country across the globe.

THE ELIXIR OF LIFE

It's probably impossible to pinpoint the exact moment when distilled alcohol was first poured into a glass and enjoyed as a social, and surely intoxicating, remedy (and we doubt in any case whether the people who did were able to remember it themselves the next day). Records dating back to ancient Egypt and China indicate that the process of distillation was used to create medicinal preparations, elixirs, and perfumes by extracting essential oils from herbs, spices, and plants rather than alcohol for consumption.

Despite modern-day advances in technology, much of the equipment employed in the production of spirits today hasn't changed a great deal over the centuries. Take the pot still, with its iconic enduring shape (*see* p.18), which was used by the ancient Greeks. In the early part of the Middle Ages, a technique known as freeze distillation was practised, where a solution was frozen to separate the alcohol from the water, but this was obviously feasible only in the coldest of countries, and even then production was sporadic.

Another benefit of distillation was that it allowed for the transportation of alcoholic beverages around the world without spoiling. In fact, the advent of distilled spirit for consumption probably hit its stride in Europe around the twelfth century, when the first brandies became more readily available. Wines were often distilled in an attempt to preserve them for long journeys, often overseas.

With the Black Death extending its formidable velvet cloak of doom across Europe in the fourteenth century, many physicians turned to distilled spirits as a way to ward off the disease, and the real essence of a national spirit was formed. At some point the Latin term *aqua vitae*, or *uisge beatha* in Scottish Gaelic, meaning "water of life", was coined, and cereals, fruits, and starchy vegetables began to form the basis of a spirit's recipe. From the distillation of whiskey in Ireland (alongside poitín or poteen), gin in Holland, vodkas in both Poland and Russia, and schnapps in Germany, many other distinctly flavoured spirits followed, each relying on the

personality of the producer and the availability of the base ingredient.

Spirits fortified both the body and the mind in times of conflict, as well as helping to act as social lubricants in times of celebration. But as we shall explore in several of the individual spirit chapters, there *is* such a concept as "too much of a good thing", and several spirits, such as gin and absinthe, took the rap for widespread social unrest.

THE BOOM IN THE DISTILLING BUSINESS...

What would unify and reaffirm spirit production, moving it away from the relative inconsistency and inefficiency that had crept into production techniques? The filing in Great Britain of Patent #5974 in 1830 and the tenacity of an Irishman called Aeneas Coffey, whose column still design took distilling to unprecedented levels (*see* p.21). His invention enabled drinks companies to produce vast quantities of spirits at a faster and more consistent rate than ever before, giving rise to large distilleries of all types around the world.

↑ Distillation may have humble origins that stretch back thousands of years, but thanks to science, the techniques have been well and truly perfected.

Spirits fortified both body and mind in times of conflict and acted as social lubricants in times of celebration.

Consider the column still design the equivalent of the motorcar as compared to the more traditional horse-and-cart copper pot still (*see* p.18). Whereas a rustic, more crafted made-in-batches approach was still very much at the heart of the production of spirits such as malt whisky, Tequila, and brandy, which relied to a greater extent on the classic pot still with its swan neck, heated from below, to develop their distinct flavours, the column still was continuous, churning out spirit in almost endless capacities. Times were very rosy (and merry) indeed.

...AND THEN THE BUST

Moving into the twentieth century, National Prohibition, which came into force in the USA on January 16, 1920, marked another huge change in the life of distilled spirits. The thriving American whiskey industry was brought to its knees almost overnight, with hundreds of distilleries ceasing to exist, their once-gleaming stills being dismantled and casks of maturing spirit senselessly poured away. And it was not just the American whiskey industry that suffered; rum, gin, and Irish and Scottish whisky producers all lost a major market, many of them closing as a result.

But clearly the thirst for spirits could not be halted simply by a change to the law. The clandestine business of making whiskey, gin, vodka, rum, and anything else the underground distiller cared to turn his hand to, continued (often at night, hence the name "moonshine") behind the backs of the US authorities, making millionaires of gangsters such as Al Capone. With consistency of production gone, the results were largely undrinkable, and in some cases they were deadly methanol-heavy concoctions.

Thankfully, the law was repealed in December 1933, but the landscape of distillation in the US and abroad was left bloodied, bruised, and sprawled across the canvas. Until recently that is.

THE LATEST CHAPTER: CRAFT SPIRIT

In the last decade, the USA has witnessed an explosion of artisanal distilleries. Each one, no matter what spirit it's producing, has been set up and is operated by like-minded individuals looking to capture their personality within their products.

According to the American Distilling Institute (ADI), established in 2003 by craft brewer and enthusiast Bill Owens to support the rights and commercial interests of craft distillers, as few as 64 existed in 2004. Now there are over 400, demonstrating that the landscape of distilling in the USA is truly thriving. A similar situation is occurring across Central Europe, with individuals, farms, small breweries, and wineries adding to their compendium of equipment by installing small copper pot stills or micro-sized column stills to create eaux-de-vie, gins, vodkas, whiskies, and brandies.

↑ An unusually shaped copper pot still. Copper is one of the most important metals used in distillation, thanks to the cleansing effects it has on a spirit.

All of this leads us to the 64,000-litre question: what defines a craft distillery? There is no definitive answer – as such. While organizations like the ADI are pushing for a legally recognized definition of a craft spirit in the USA, it is unlikely that any specific law will ever apply internationally, which gives the whole nature of craft/artisanal/small-batch (delete as appropriate) distilling the air of unconventionality and unpredictability it truly needs to maintain its vibrancy and independence.

To qualify for entry into this book, there are no rules on size, product type, or historical provenance. Honesty, innovation, passion, flair within flavour, and a clear expression of personality are the key criteria. And there has never been a period in the history of distilling during which all these have been more lovingly bottled.

WHAT IS A

—

Spirit?

This is the point in the book where we get into some science. Hang on, don't run away! This isn't going to be like school. You don't have to open your notebook or put on some safety goggles – far from it, in fact. Don't forget that we are still talking about booze, which makes this more like university than school: just without the debt at the end of it.

A spirit is a distilled beverage with a significant level of alcohol, usually 20% alcohol by volume (ABV) or above, and unsweetened (although brandies and rums are allowed some added sweetness). Certain spirits, such as whisky, insist on a minimum of 40% ABV, and many have a much higher alcohol content – some up to 80%. But where does this important aspect, the alcohol, actually come from? How is it produced?

Well, it's all down to our new best friend: yeast. In the right conditions, alcohol is made when yeast is combined with any substance that contains starches or sugars. This process is known as anaerobic respiration or, to give it its more familiar name, fermentation, with the yeast breaking down sugars into carbon dioxide and alcohol. One of the key facts to remember here is that the alcohol can be produced from any base product containing sugar or starch.

However, a spirit is not just about the process of making alcohol; that is *brewing*. A spirit is a level up from a brew – the PhD of the drinks world – and to achieve this higher accolade, you need a process called distillation.

TYPES OF

Distillation

Put simply, distillation is separation, specifically of liquids and vapours. It is used all over the world in laboratories to make some of the most integral parts of your life, including purified water and perfumes and oils. But when it comes to making spirits, it's all about separating, or liberating, alcohol from water, and there are a few different ways in which this can be done.

The first and most traditional way is simply to heat up the brew (*see* pp.16–18). Both the water and the alcohol vaporize simultaneously, but the alcohol is more volatile so it is enriched more quickly than the water in the condensate (the result of condensation). As it turns into a vapour, it leaves some of the water behind, but now it needs to be captured, and this is done simply by removing the energy from the alcohol to form a liquid again. The name given to this part of the process is "condensing".

Once the first distillation has been completed, there will still be some water that made the journey too. To raise the "proof" of it – to decrease the ratio of water to alcohol – the process can be repeated, often over and over again. There is no set rule

as to how many times a spirit is distilled, with single malt Scotch whisky commonly distilled twice, and vodka frequently being distilled up to four or five times.

Within this heating method there are two commonly used methods: pot still distilling and continuous distilling.

POT DISTILLING

The use of pot stills is the more traditional way to distil. These are basically copper kettles that funnel into a tight neck at the top, allowing for the alcohol vapours to be condensed and carried away to a spirit receiver.

In the early days of distilling, these items would have been small, portable, and agricultural, giving farmers an alternative use for their produce. However, pot stills are now mostly static

and employed on a large scale at distilleries across the world. By way of example, just one of the stills at The Glenlivet single malt Scotch whisky distillery in Scotland has a capacity of 15,500 litres (3,400 gallons) – not something you would want to move around on the back of a John Deere.

Despite the large capacity of some pot stills and the distilleries that use them, one wouldn't consider them to be "industrial" in their production. This is partly due to their traditional nature and partly due to the fact that distilleries that use pot stills produce their spirit in distinct batches. But the main reason for their status as an artisanal production method is the contrast they have with their younger sibling, the column or continuous still.

CONTINUOUS OR COLUMN DISTILLING

Having been developed during the Industrial Revolution (it was registered as a patent in 1830) and refined from previous designs, the column still (also known as the continuous or patent still, or Coffey still after its designer, Aeneas Coffey) allows for vast volumes of alcohol to be manufactured from a base brew.

In short, these stills are designed to replicate heating and condensing of spirit a huge number of times in succession, eliminating the need for batches and creating a fast and continuous flow of alcohol – hence "continuous" still. Dwarfing their pot still relations, distilleries with column stills are humongous. For example, the Cameronbridge Distillery in Scotland uses column stills to produce 100 million litres (22 million gallons) of grain whisky for some of the world's most well-known blends, and 40 million litres (880,000 gallons) of alcohol destined for several best-selling vodka and gin brands – a simply staggering amount.

Telling the difference between a pot still and a column still is easy. A copper pot still is like a small cottage, in contrast to the skyscraper stature of a column still, often so tall that that they need to be situated on the outside of their production facilities, making their premises look like Lloyds of London.

↑ *Science fiction distillation. Some column stills appear to have been the product of Jules Verne's imagination.*

With all this talk of heating up and separation, it's time to chill out a bit and look at the other, rarer form of distillation: vacuum or cold distilling.

VACUUM OR COLD DISTILLATION

Now, we said this wasn't school and that this isn't a science textbook, so we are going to spare you the detailed physics behind vacuum distillation, but we will tell you its advantage: no extreme heat is applied during the process, which is why it's called "cold distillation". Instead, a vacuum is created that enables the alcohol to turn to vapour more readily. With no extra heat present, it could be argued that a better result is achieved when creating a spirit that is flavoured during distillation, causing less damage to the flavour compounds of the often delicate botanicals used.

DIY DISTILLING – A NO-NO

It might seem pretty simple stuff, all this: taking some low-alcohol brew, heating it up, and condensing the vapour. But if you're looking to try distilling at home, be warned! Not only is distilling without a licence illegal in many countries, it is also highly flammable and, if done incorrectly, can make you go blind. The potential for the latter hazard depends on which of the two main types of alcohol are being produced: methanol or ethanol.

Methanol is the bad type. This is the kid in the playground who you are not allowed to hang around with, or the apple on the tree you shouldn't eat. To be blunt: AVOID! Ethanol, on the other hand, is the gold in this alchemistic process, the one item we want to keep, and it is just this skill of separating the good alcohol from the bad that makes distilling a real art form. In summary, don't try this at home, or you could simply turn to our "How to make your own house gin" section (*see* pp.38–9) – it's your choice, really.

TWO COLOURFUL CHARACTERS

White & Dark

For the professional distiller, however, whichever form of distillation they choose to use, the resulting spirit will always be clear in colour. But as you peruse the spirits selection in your local bar, you will notice that some spirits have colour to them. That's because there are two distinct categories of spirit: white and dark.

White spirits are just that – anything that is fresh off the still, gin and vodka being the best examples.

Dark spirits are those that have been matured in wood, often in oak casks, although some other wood types are occasionally used, such as chestnut and cherry wood, for a period of time. It is this "maturation" that gives colour and flavour to the spirit. Maturation times can vary wildly and depend upon a number of factors: from the style of the base spirit through to the size of the barrels and even the temperature and atmosphere in a warehouse.

For example, some brandies or particular whiskies may mature for upwards of 30 or 40 years, imbibing flavour, complexity, and colour as each day passes. However, take the same spirit and the same barrel and move it to, say, India, then as the cask slumbers in the Indian heat, part of the contents will evaporate very quickly indeed. It is estimated that casks maturing in hot climates lose around 10 per cent of their volume per year (affectionately known as the "angels' share"), whereas in cooler climes, such as Scotland, the same effect results in around a two per-cent loss.

It doesn't take a mathematician to work out that the whisky in our Indian barrel will soon disappear entirely, in contrast to Scotland where it can slowly mature for a long period of time. This doesn't make Scotch better than Indian malt whisky; it just makes it different. And this is what we are here to celebrate: the alternative spirits, the hidden gems. That's the true spirit of this book.

How to Sample a Spirit

The spirits we feature in this book have been lovingly prepared, often by a passionate independent producer or by someone who is at the very top of their game and who understands flavour and production methods.

It is true to say that most producers of these spirits will also be open-minded as to how you choose to consume them, be it neat as a nightcap or composed into a cocktail. For them it's simply "job done" that you are enjoying their creations in one form or another. But before you throw ice into your tumbler or a large measure into your Manhattan, it's crucial to understand the intrinsic flavours of the spirit that you are about to imbibe.

OUR THREE-STAGE REVIEWING PROCESS

When we are looking at a spirit to determine where it sits in relation to other products in the category, and also to see how it will work in a cocktail or a long drink with a mixer, we employ a three-stage process.

The first stage is to study the aroma of the drink. Known in the business as the "nose", it is this element that is your very first flavour introduction to the spirit. What rises from the glass is important – first impressions last, and all that. And here comes the first of our tips: if you are serious about understanding the aromas in your spirits, buy yourself a nosing glass. Typically, these are tulip-shaped so that the aromas are funnelled up and out of the glass. If you don't own one, you can use a Champagne flute, which has a similar effect. If you don't own a Champagne flute, you clearly haven't celebrated enough in life.

Now for the second stage. Once you have poured a measure of your chosen spirit, lift your glass towards your nose, and when it's about 2.5cm (1in) away, stop! Here it's good to remember that we are dealing with high-strength alcohol spirit in excess of 20% alcohol by volume, mostly over 40% ABV and sometimes as high as 60, 70, or even 80% ABV. These are spirits that go to 11. As a result, at the higher end of the ABV spectrum, the first aroma that will hit your nose is… ethanol. Hidden behind the alcohol is where the delicate flavours are, and uncovering them is the key. On the whole, the higher-strength alcohol spirits will have been designed that way. Just as a big car needs a big engine, often a spirit full of flavour will need a good percentage of alcohol to pull it through.

The counterbalance to this is twofold. Firstly, and this is a very simple tip, as you look down on top of the glass, think of the rim as a clock face with 12 o'clock pointing directly away from you and 6 o'clock closest to you. What you should find when tilting the glass towards you and nosing, is that at 12 o'clock you'll find much less of the alcohol and more of the flavours than if you nose at 6 o'clock. Conversely, at the bottom of the glass you will find the heavier tones, which can often mask the true, delicate flavours. Secondly, to tame the alcohol levels you can simply add some water. Our advice is to use still spring water for the purest effect, but if you don't have any, then tap water will do just fine.

Before we move on to the third stage, let's introduce the idea that the process of nosing and tasting a spirit is a little like going to the movies…

1.
The Trailer
Nosing the spirit is like watching the trailer for a film. It will give you an idea about what to expect but it won't give the whole game away and you won't have picked up the full narrative. What it will reveal, however, is whether the spirit is engaging enough to take a sip. We have all seen trailers at the cinema and thought, "Meh… not for me. Next!"

2.
The Film Itself
The second stage, sampling the flavour – tasting the stuff – is like going to the cinema to see the movie. As you slowly sip your spirit, take some time to assess the flavours. In the same way as watching a great film, ask yourself whether the plot flows smoothly. Do the personalities of the main characters come across fully? Do you fancy the leading actor? If this is an old whisky or Cognac, it may have spent decades in a cask maturing, waiting for the right moment to be bottled. Don't go swigging it back; savour. Enjoy. You don't watch a movie at home on fast forward. Don't do the same with your spirits.

3.
The Post-Movie In-Depth Discussion
After you have submerged your taste-buds and swallowed the lot (and you would be in welcome company if you decided to make notes and keep a tasting record), you'll get the third stage, known as "the finish". This relates to the flavours that linger after you have swallowed, and it's like the conversation with your mates down the pub after the film is over. Did you enjoy it? What style of film was it? Was it as good as other work from the same producer – are you on the internet message boards looking for answers to the cliffhanger? More importantly, would it inspire you to take another sip, or, to use the film analogy shamelessly again, pop back into the cinema for a second viewing? The nose, the taste, and the finish are the "Holy Trinity" for assessing the spirits in this book. In our opinion, every spirit featured is an Oscar-winning performance – and most are certainly not a straight-to-DVD flop!

10

Essential (Non-booze) Items for a Cocktail Cabinet

1.
SHAKER

If you want to play at being James Bond, this is an essential for your cabinet. There are various classic cocktails that require a vigorous shake to mix the ingredients. Just don't get over-confident with your shake, as if you fail to hold the cocktail shaker correctly, you will find that your living room walls resemble a Jackson Pollock painting when the lid flies off. There are two main types of cocktail shaker: the Boston shaker, which consists of two halves, one metal and one glass, both of equal size (a separate strainer is required for these); and the cobbler shaker, which looks like a New York fire hydrant and comes in three parts, often all metal. (The first part is a large compartment for ingredients. The second is the lid, which has a built-in strainer. The third is a cap, which often doubles as a measure.)

However, maybe you are visiting a friend and want to mix up a shaken cocktail but you find that you are stuck for a cocktail shaker, in which case you can use a number of other items, so long as they have a lid. We have been known to whip up a mean Whiskey Sour using a Kilner jar at certain parties devoid of any cocktail-making equipment. Just because there are specialist tools designed for making cocktails doesn't mean you *can't* make them without these items. Just pick some ingredients and go for it.

2.
STRAINER

The clue is in the name with this bad boy. An essential piece of kit in serving shaken cocktails for straining off excess ice and other items such as fruit or citrus zests while you pour the cocktail from a shaker into your chosen glassware. If you are using a cobbler shaker (*see* left), your strainer will be built in.

3.
MEASURES

A lot of cocktail recipes will tell you the different measures required for each component, and it's essential that these guidelines are adhered to in terms of their ratio to one another. This is not, however, a science lab, nor a bakery, and you will often see seasoned bartenders "free pour" the liquid parts of their cocktails without even so much as a glance at a measure. Although at home it's good to use measures initially to construct your cocktails, since mixing a cocktail is as much an art as it is a science, you should use a straw to taste your cocktail once it has been made, and if it requires a little more or a little less of an ingredient, then adjust your mix accordingly.

4.
MUDDLER

A large wooden stick reminiscent of a miniature Victorian rolling pin. Its job is to crush ingredients such as mint, herbs, and citrus fruit to release their flavours before mixing and/or shaking.

5.
SUGAR SYRUP

Yum! A very simple ingredient that is vital for adding sweetness to cocktails. Almost as important to the barkeep as salt is to the chef, sugar syrup is just sugar dissolved in water. You can buy this inexpensively (Monin is the leading brand, offering various flavoured sugar syrups such as gingerbread and vanilla; you will know them from popular high-street coffee shops, which stock a range to flavour their coffees), but it is so simple to make and allows experimentation with different types of sugar. Simply dissolve white sugar in boiling water using half the amount of water to sugar. Let it cool and then store in a clean, well-sealed glass bottle in a cool place. A batch will last a few weeks. For a bit of extra sweetness, try making a syrup with demerara sugar.

6.
BAR SPOON

A bar spoon has many uses, the first being the alternative to shaking some drinks. A good stir will often be enough to mix your drink if it doesn't require shaking. Pouring carbonated or other fizzy liquids over the back of an upturned bar spoon is also a useful way to disperse the ingredient into the glass and can be an effective method of "layering" drinks into a glass.

7.
BITTERS

Bitters! So important we have a whole chapter on them. Use them to "pimp" your cocktail and add some really interesting, unusual, and intense flavours. For more information, *see* pp.212–17.

8.
ICE

The majority of cocktails need chilling and ice is the best way to do this. If you get into making cocktails, you will go through a LOT of ice, from prefilling glasses to chill them and using ice in the shaker, to the actual ice needed for the drink itself; that's already three handfuls of ice for one drink, so this is not something that you can achieve with a small freezer compartment and a single ice tray from IKEA. Nope, you're gonna need heaps of the stuff and possibly even a dedicated freezer for storing Martini glasses and bags of ice. Ice can be purchased from your local supermarket, and if you choose to buy in bulk, make sure you choose the variety made with pure spring water. If you want to make ice at home, nip down to your local homeware store and get plenty of ice trays, then freeze bottled spring water or boiled tap water (for additional purification). If you are feeling brave, fill a few old ice-cream tubs with spring water and use these, along with an ice pick, to provide your ice needs for an entire evening. Just be careful when drinking strong cocktails while using an ice pick – you only have 10 fingers, you know.

9.
ZESTER OR PEELER

Many cocktails require either zesty fruits in them (and let's not forget the golden rule here that lemons are sour and limes are bitter) or other decorations and garnishes. These are easy to obtain with the use of a zester or a peeler. For ease of zesting, go for a standard speed peeler. Again, sharp instruments are best used before, not after, a couple of cocktails. Cherries are occasionally required for classic cocktails such as the Old Fashioned, and these can be purchased in jars. Steer clear of cheap glacé-style cherries and use only good, well-marinated maraschino cherries or, for a truly great experience, Griottines – cherries marinated in kirsch, a teaspoonful of which will add an extra level of flavour to any Old Fashioned.

10.
TOWEL

A clean bar is a happy bar, so get yourself a good bar towel or tea towel. For an extra-professional look, wear it hanging out of your back trouser pocket.

GIN

A Botanical Bonanza

SPIRIT NAME	ETYMOLOGY/ COUNTRY OF ORIGIN	COLOUR	MAIN COUNTRIES OF PRODUCTION	BIGGEST-SELLING GLOBAL BRANDS	KEY INGREDIENTS
Gin. Widely regarded as being derived from the word "juniper", or *genièvre* in French, or *jenever* in Dutch.	Holland. First used as a medicine in the late sixteenth century, then as a widely consumed spirit by the seventeenth century.	Generally clear, although some infused or compounded gins carry a slight hue, and cask-aged gins, although rare, develop colour over time.	The Netherlands, UK, USA, Spain, India, the Philippines, France, and Germany.	Ginebra San Miguel, Larios, Beefeater, Tanqueray, Seagram's, Gordon's, Gilbey's, Blue Riband, and Gibson's.	Neutral grain or, in some cases, grape spirit, either redistilled or infused predominantly with juniper berries and a variety of other herbs and botanical flavours.

GIN

A Botanical Bonanza

Gin is globally one of the most popular spirits, making inroads into almost every country in the world that consumes alcohol. From sachets of gin supped neat on street corners in Nigeria to Ginebra San Miguel, which sells over 200 million bottles a year (mainly in its home market of the Philippines), gin is seriously big business. "Heritage" brands such as Gordon's, Beefeater, and Tanqueray, which have been around since the 1800s, are now universally recognized names and a consistent pour on speed-rails worldwide.

Gin is enjoyed in many forms, be it simply mixed with tonic or stirred in a Martini. But what exactly is gin, this clear spirit that is so voraciously imbibed around the globe? At its most straightforward, gin is a distilled spirit flavoured with juniper berries and any other botanicals or herbs to add to the taste. But there is a lot more to understanding gin than just juniper. The location, the production technique, the balance of juniper with botanicals and herbs, even cask ageing nowadays... there is plenty to get your teeth into when it comes to gin.

"LONDON DRY" AS IN STYLE, NOT CITY

To start with, we should tackle what exactly is meant when we see the words "London Dry" on a bottle of gin. Unlike Scotch whisky or Cognac, London Dry gin can be made anywhere in the world. "London Dry" is a reference to the style of gin production rather than an indication of its genealogy. Considered the highest level of gin-making, London Dry is the term used for gin made by including fresh botanicals and juniper berries in the distillation, or redistillation, of the product.

We say "redistillation" because most gin houses don't actually make the alcohol or spirit from the start. Producing alcohol is a pretty tricky process (*see* pp.20–1) and the secret of the gin distiller is in their particular recipe.

London Dry gin is traditionally distilled in copper pot stills (*see* p.20) with botanicals and juniper berries chucked into the mix. As the spirit distils and evaporates upwards, it takes with it the flavours from orange peel, liquorice, cassia bark, coco nibs, or whatever other ingredients have been added.

Once the distillation has run its course, the gin-maker is left with a slew of liquid and botanicals in the bottom of his still, which often goes on to be put to other uses. For example, the head distiller at the City of London Distillery sends his to a local London brewer, who uses it in the mash bill (the mix of base ingredients used in brewing or distilling) for a summer ale, cunningly called "Gin".

Not all London Dry gins actually add their botanical mix into the boiling section of their pot stills. Some, like Bombay Sapphire for instance, hang a basket of botanicals in the upper reaches of their copper pots, allowing the distilled vapour to pass through them. This is believed to result in a lighter flavour of gin, and is still classed within the London Dry style.

NEW GIN ON THE BLOCK

We now know that London Dry gin can be made anywhere in the world so long as the botanical mix is included in the distillation, but there are other ways to make gin where the flavouring is added post-distillation. Hendrick's gin, a new boy on the market developed by owner William Grant & Sons in 1999, is made in Scotland at the Girvan Distillery south of Glasgow. It has certain distinctive elements in its flavour, including those provided by its famous key ingredients of cucumber and rose petal, added after its initial distillation. As a result, Hendrick's can't use the moniker London Dry.

↓ *In its early days, gin was a spirit that united all classes, creeds, and, unlike today, ages.* →*Individual botanicals are often distilled to check for quality at the Sipsmith distillery in London.*

CASK-AGEING GIN

Gin is a white spirit and designed to be clear in appearance, but some producers have been experimenting with ageing gin in cask. This is done in whisky and brandy production, where wood has always been used to give the spirits flavour, and in Tequila, where some of the spirit is allowed to "rest" in oak (*see* p.73). Commercially available aged gins are rare, however, with one major brand, Beefeater, taking the leap in 2013 with its first such offering. Other producers of cask-aged gins include FEW Spirits and Professor Cornelius Ampleforth. The additional flavours that the wood imparts can really add something different to the traditional juniper-based varieties, but be warned: lengthy maturation will result in a smothering of gin's delicate flavours.

A TALE OF DUTCH COURAGE

Despite being one of the best-known drinks in the world, gin is often associated with London, partly due to the moniker "London Dry" on a gin bottle label (*see* p.34). However, gin is actually about as English as Chinese tea, having first been imported to the UK from Europe in the seventeenth century.

Gin's story begins in the Dutch Republic during the early 1600s, where a juniper-flavoured spirit was commonly used as a diuretic medicine. However, even before anyone had thought about mixing this drink with tonic and ice, let alone a slice of cucumber, the Dutch had established their own distillery making juniper-flavoured spirit, and a brand that is still around today was born. Bols, the distillery which is recorded as having been set up in Amsterdam in 1575, remains a widely distributed and consumed product around the world, making it the longest-surviving distilled drinks brand in history. Not a gin as we would know it, Bols is classed as a

> → *Gin is no longer a crude spirit, but is made in the most highly scientific of ways.*

genever or jenever and, with such a rich history, is a world away from many of the new brands of gin we see populating our shelves today.

The arrival in London of what was to become known as gin was due to an unlikely source: the British Army. In the late 1500s, scores of troops were sent from Britain to be stationed in Europe, ending up with their involvement in support of the Dutch during the Thirty Years War (1618–48). Here, the troops discovered genever and its interesting flavours, and took an instant liking to this unusual spirit.

Gin's story begins in the Dutch Republic during the early 1600s, where a juniper-flavoured spirit was commonly being used as a diuretic medicine.

It was the use of a juniper-flavoured spirit as fortification before battle that gave rise to the term "Dutch courage", still used today for those in need of a small motivational kick. We find a deadline much more useful than a shot of spirit to get us going, and we are sure you have your alternative motivational tools, but for these unlucky souls, the sharp end of a bayonet was their only other option, so a small nip of alcohol seems much more preferable.

These troops brought their top tipple back to England after the war and, deep into the 1600s, it was a Dutchman who took control of the British throne. The nobility, keen to find favour with the Dutch king, began to consume his native spirit. This, coupled with the ease of production, allowed the drink to gain a firm foothold with the English drinker.

Further to the fashion of the day, the British Parliament created a hothouse environment for the growth of gin when it passed the Distilling Act in 1690. This encouraged the activity by enabling pretty much anyone who so fancied to begin distilling the spirit. By 1694, any individual who wished to distil simply needed to post a notice of intention outside his or her property, giving a fair warning of 10 days before starting up. No think-tanks or marketing men here. Nor was this "make do and mend" – this was "make gin and vend".

>> 5

*Indipensable
gin facts*

1 No matter how many
   botanicals are used, juniper
   must be the overriding flavour
   in a gin.
2 London Dry gin doesn't have
   to be made in London.
3 The exact botanical recipe
   in a gin brand is usually a
   time-honoured and very
   closely guarded secret known
   only by a select few.
4 The Filipinos are the largest
   consumers of gin in the world.
5 William Hogarth's famous
   1751 painting *Gin Lane*
   was actually a wickedly
   satirical piece of propaganda,
   supposedly commissioned by
   London's ailing breweries.

GONE TO RACK & MOTHER'S RUIN

Such was the problem of home-produced gin
in London in the early 1700s that it gained the
nicknames "mother's ruin" and "Madam Geneva".
As the price of gin dipped below those of beer
and ale, the drink became even more popular,
especially with the poor. It is estimated that a
staggering 40 million litres (9 million gallons) –
or an even more eye-watering 90 bottles for every
adult resident of the city – was being consumed
per year at that time.

It was in 1751 that gin became the subject
of one of the most famous works of art from
that period of time, William Hogarth's *Gin Lane*
(*see* above). In his work, Hogarth depicts a scene
from the streets of London where the community
is ravaged by illness, living in squalor, hungry, and
dying. He contrasts the engraving with another,
Beer Street, that shows men and women happy,
jolly, and full of life.

HOW TO MAKE YOUR
OWN HOUSE GIN

Yet another way of producing
a juniper-flavoured spirit is by
simply soaking juniper berries
in high-strength, neutral
alcohol. This process is known as
compounding and is very much
something you can do at home,
if the licensing laws in your
country or state allow. All you
need is your own unique recipe

GIN GOES GLOBAL

In the years that followed, many now-household names in gin were born. The major distilleries of Gordon's, Plymouth, Tanqueray, and Beefeater allowed for a consistent and high-quality product, and exported their gins around the world to established key markets such as the USA, which remain vibrant today.

But it wasn't just London that welcomed gin with open arms. Countries as diverse as Spain and the Philippines, home to the world's biggest gin brand, Ginebra San Miguel, began drinking gin in abundance.

Mixed simply with tonic or poured into a Martini glass with a dash of dry vermouth, gin is the foundation of some of the most simple yet flavoursome cocktails ever devised. From Southeast Asia's Singapore Sling to the Italian-born Negroni, via

↑ *Waxed bottle tops have seen a growth recently, along with classic gin styles.*

James Bond's reinvention of the Martini in the more potent form of the Vesper, gin established itself as central to the emerging cocktail culture of the 1800s and is still standing strong today.

The Gin and Tonic was originally designed to ward off malaria in hot countries, notably those that were being enveloped by the ever-expanding British Empire, such as India. Its popularity, along with mixing, has helped gin's story to echo through the ages.

Born in Europe and educated in London, gin is now off conquering the world, and today it is experiencing something of a renaissance, with new gins popping up all over the globe, from Italy to the Scottish island of Islay. London is still a major player in the game, with the Beefeater Distillery, formerly the only producer left in the city, being joined by the City of London Distillery (COLD), Sipsmith, The London Distillery Company, and Thames Distillers, and whose brands easily outnumber this short list of producers.

Gin has shown itself to stand the test of time. Currently there seems to be no stopping it.

of juniper and other selected botanicals, herbs, and spices and some natural spirit – you can use commercially produced bottles of vodka if you like.

Once you have made sure that the botanicals you are using are actually edible and are not going to kill you (this isn't *Into the Wild*), simply stick them in a demi-john, soak, and remove. How long you do this for is up to you – just keep a close eye

(– nose, and tongue) on the infusing spirit, as it probably won't need long. And that's it. You have your own house gin. It might not look great, probably having picked up some colour and some, erm, "floaty bits" from your botanicals, but by golly it's yours.

Jump on your computer and put together your own label, using the same ABV strength as your original base spirit, print

off, and apply to a clean bottle or jam jar. Bottle the gin by passing it through a coffee filter, secure the cap or lid to your bottle or jar, stick it in your freezer, and delight your guests with your own house gin whenever they pop over for a quick gin Martini – *see* p.40 for our suggested recipe. Just don't water it down – gin has to be over 37.5% ABV in Europe and 40% ABV in the USA to be called gin.

OUR GUIDE *to the* PERFECT

Gin Martini

Thankfully, making this most sophisticated of cocktails requires very little preparation and few ingredients. But best of all, the Martini allows your gin to show its true character. Our all-time favourite Martini gin is No.3 London Dry Gin, which has no tomfoolery in the botanicals department, just a hearty juniper note back-dropped by cardamom, lemon peel, and a little spice.

1.

Store a Martini glass and your chosen gin in the freezer. Due to the high levels of alcohol, the gin won't freeze, but it will take on a wonderful syrupy texture as it chills. Placing the glass and gin in the freezer means that you will be serving your friends the best cocktail they have ever had.

2.

When you are ready to serve the drink, simply wash the glass out with a little dry vermouth and pour in at least 50ml (2 measures) of the chilled gin. The mix of gin and vermouth can also be stirred down with ice first, before being poured into your chilled Martini glass. But don't employ a shaker; leave that to fictional spies.

3.

For additional oily body, top off the gin with an olive or add our choice: a delicate twist of fresh lemon zest.

4.

Have the number for a local taxi company at hand. Trust us: if you make more than one of these for your guests, they'll certainly need it.

Just the tonic
Our guide to four of the best

We've all been there, we're sure: it's mid- to late afternoon, the working day resigned to history. Overhead, a bright blue sky remains, providing the perfect backdrop for a sun still hard at work, asserting its power and authority over a scorched land.

In the middle of all this is you, a book resting on your lap, a copy of the daily newspaper at your feet, as you are sprawled across the ground soaking up the sun. As you take in the view, you feel a thirst for something refreshing yet with a kick, and there is only one truly refreshing drink to fill that role: a Gin and Tonic.

We have aimed in this book on spirits to help you to understand them more and to give you alternative options to the major brands' standard offerings. However, when it comes to G&T, we are looking at a true partnership. The Lennon and McCartney of drinks, Gin and Tonic are excellent on their own but exceptional together.

As it is a partnership, when you make a Gin and Tonic, you should not only consider the gin you use but also the type and integrity of tonic water. How often are we burdened with an opened bottle of tonic left idling in the fridge, long since freed of its zeal and panache, that will only produce flat, second-rate results?

If this situation sounds familiar, consider the following option: forego your usual litre-bottle purchase and pick up your tonic in miniature canned or small-bottle form. Besides having a constant supply of youthful tonic, you will never again hear that depressing "phhuff" sound as you unscrew a week-old bottle.

But back to the quality of the tonic. This is a market that has exploded in the past decade, giving consumers across the globe access to a much higher quality of tonic, and therefore G&T, than was previously within their grasp. So here are a select few brands of tonic worth seeking out to extract the very most from this classic combination drink:

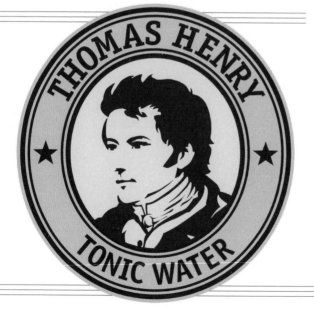

← *Full of hot air? Thomas Henry was credited with inventing carbonated drinks.*

FRANKLIN & SONS LTD

A blend of natural cinchona bark extract from Ecuador, British spring water and sugar beet. This isn't as sweet as other tonics, allowing for the gin's flavours to come through.

1724

With its origins from high in the Andes (1,724m/5,656ft high to be precise), where quinine bark was apparently first discovered, this is a masculine, woody tonic that pairs very well with robust, high-strength gins for a particularly heady combo.

FOUR
OF
THE
BEST

FEVER-TREE

With the saccharine sweetness of most mainstream brands of tonic dialled down, Fever-Tree harnesses the biting astringency of natural ingredients to give your G&T real authenticity.

THOMAS HENRY

As with Fever-Tree, Thomas Henry embraces the natural bitterness of quinine, creating a tonic water that is robust and uncompromising in its flavour.

Botanicals & Their Properties

We know that the key to making gin is to add flavour through the medium of botanicals. But how do you stop gin from being just juniper juice, and which botanicals will add the flavours we all know and love? All gin distillers have their own secret recipe, some using herbs and spices from their own backyard, others from far-flung places.

JUNIPER: THE PRICKLY KIND

Juniper, the key ingredient, is a funny beast. It grows wild rather than being cultivated and therefore is the one element that gin distillers have no control over. The berry is sourced mainly from the Tuscany region of Italy, and the juniper bushes are harvested around October time by the locals, who grab the thorny branches and hit them with a stick so that the berries fall off. It's a hard game because each branch contains three years' worth of growth at the same time. This means that if you bash too hard, you will knock off next year's berries and the year's after that as well. You can't cut the branch off, as you will lose the whole branch and next year's berries too. And no juniper means no gin – a very bad thing indeed.

Juniper berries vary in their aromatic properties. At the Beefeater Distillery, each year they choose just five batches of juniper from a tasting of over 500.

Other key botanicals that are often used in gin production can be seen on our Gin Botanical Flavour Map (*see* opposite).

> ↑ *The heart and soul of every gin: juniper berries.*

GIN BOTANICAL FLAVOUR MAP

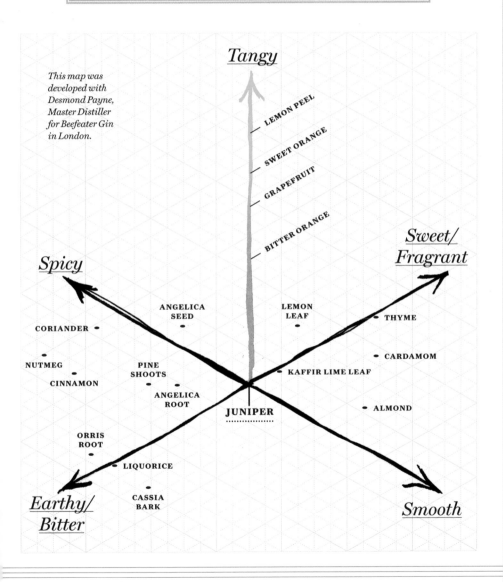

This map was developed with Desmond Payne, Master Distiller for Beefeater Gin in London.

Tangy

LEMON PEEL

SWEET ORANGE

GRAPEFRUIT

BITTER ORANGE

Sweet/ Fragrant

Spicy

ANGELICA SEED

LEMON LEAF

THYME

CORIANDER

NUTMEG

CARDAMOM

CINNAMON

PINE SHOOTS

KAFFIR LIME LEAF

ANGELICA ROOT

ALMOND

JUNIPER

ORRIS ROOT

LIQUORICE

Earthy/ Bitter

CASSIA BARK

Smooth

Meet the Maverick

» IAN HART
SACRED DISTILLERY, HIGHGATE, LONDON

From his family home in Highgate, North London, distiller Ian Hart has created a distillery that resembles no other, turning his entire dining room into a mini gin-production line. At the Hart household, it's always gin o'clock.

Can you tell us where the name of the distillery comes from?
"Our two signature products, Sacred Gin [*see* p.48] and London Dry Vodka, each contain a small amount of the highest-grade frankincense, for which the Latin name is *Boswellia sacra*. This is an nod or a reference to some of the earliest London Dry gins that used to augment their juniper with other woods such as pine and oak – probably because juniper was not available in abundance. The resinous note of frankincense complements the juniper."

Your production methods are very different to other gin producers – can you explain in a nutshell how the process works?
"Each of the organically sourced botanicals, including fresh whole citrus, is macerated separately for four to six weeks minimum with no air contact in English wheat spirit at 50% ABV. This is a seriously long time and, as a result, they retain all of their individual character and depth. However, the botanicals are not distilled in a traditional pot still but in glassware under vacuum. Vacuum distillation means that air is sucked out of the glassware with a vacuum pump, which reduces the pressure so that distillation occurs at a much lower temperature (35–45°C/ 95–113°F) than pot distillation (85–95°C/185–203°F). Because the temperature of distillation

is dramatically lower than the temperature of traditional pot distillation, the distillates are lusher and fresher – think of high-temperature-cooked marmalade flavour versus

fresh-cut oranges. The botanicals are then blended to create Sacred Gin. The result is a fresh, almost creamy, beautifully balanced gin like no other."

What's your ethos in making new spirits?
"We are always experimenting and have a library of 70–80 different kinds of botanical distillates to draw from, but the only products we bring to market are those that complement existing products. For example, as we were already producing Sacred Gin and Sacred Spiced English Vermouth, we realized that if we created an English alternative to Campari, it would be possible to make a Sacred Negroni. As a result, we developed Sacred Rosehip Cup, which is fruitier and less bitter than Campari but makes a great Negroni and is also made entirely with natural ingredients – no artificial colours, for example."

What's your biggest discovery since building a distillery?
"Spent cardamom pods and star anise make a fantastic mulch for flower beds!"

What's next for Sacred?
"To gently hit our production ceiling – we still have plenty of capacity without needing to move out of our house in Highgate."

Describe Sacred Gin in three words.
"Brilliantly homemade spirit."

» 10
GINS TO TRY

With highly characteristic botanicals giving every gin a unique aromatic fingerprint, the world of gin production has become an extremely fragrant place. Despite many well-known gin brands using the moniker of London Dry, there is actually no legal stipulation that they have to be produced in London at all, and the booming numbers of craft gin distilleries across Central Europe and North America show that gin has become seriously hot property everywhere, from Australia to the Hebridean islands.

» BOMBAY SAPPHIRE STAR OF BOMBAY
47.5% | Hampshire, England

Bombay Sapphire, with its distinctive blue bottle, is produced in the beautiful surroundings of Laverstoke Mill. Star of Bombay is a punchy, cracker of a gin, big on juniper, coriander and also bergamot, bringing added intensity to a G&T. Make sure you pay a visit to the distillery – the glasshouse is a thing of unadulterated beauty.

» SACRED GIN
40% | London, England

Ian Hart has created a commercial distillery in his kitchen in North London's leafy Highgate (see pp.46–7). Distilled in a vacuum using scientific-looking glass stills, Sacred's mixture of 12 botanicals, including juniper, orange, lime, and lemon peel, cardamom, and the unusual frankincense Boswellia sacra (hence the name), has very dry, earthy notes and aromatic warming spices. The frankincense is prominent, giving this a very direct and distinct character.

» THE BOTANIST ISLAY DRY GIN
46% | Isle of Islay, Scotland

Famed for its peated single malt Scotch, the Bruichladdich Distillery on Islay bought itself a gin still, named it Ugly Betty, and now produces the highly complex Botanist. Bursting at the seams with 31 botanicals – including 22 foraged from around the island, such as bog myrtle, heather, and gorse flowers – it has a distinctly floral aroma, with classic juniper dryness in the background and a unique creaminess on the palate.

» KI NO BI KYOTO DRY GIN
45.7% | Japan

Established in Kyoto in 2016 as the first dedicated craft gin distillery in Japan, the Kyoto Distillery presents Ki No Bi, a bold yet classically styled gin, with luscious herbaceous juniper, but also distinctive Japanese notes of yuzu, hinoki (an incense-like wood) and sansho pepper. Make sure you say *kampai* with a Ki No Bi Martini in your hand!

» HERNÖ OLD TOM GIN
43% | Sweden

Hernö's rise in success can be traced to the almost fanatical dedication to gin of its founder, Jon Hillgren, who built the distillery in the leafy village of Dala in Ångermanland, northern Sweden, in 2011. Jon's take on Old Tom, a sweeter style dating back to the gin palace culture of London in the 1800s, is bold, rich and full of juniper. Outstanding stuff.

» COTSWOLDS DRY GIN
46% | Shipston-on-Stour, England

Founder Dan Szor set out to make English whisky, and gin production began purely to fill the time they were waiting for the whisky to mature. However, the recipe they created turned out to be a hit – now there is equal focus on producing all of their fantastic distillates. With a big, oily palate of lavender, bay leaf, grapefruit and lime, this gin makes a brilliant G&T.

» EAST LONDON LIQUOR COMPANY BARREL-AGED GIN
43% | London, England

Perhaps the most exciting craft distillery in London at the moment, East London Liquor Company (ELLCo.) has revolutionized the capital's gin scene. What's more, they've started a nifty barrel ageing programme, whereby different cask types are used to mature and round off the gin for up to a year: French oak, American bourbon and white wine casks give each batch a distinctive, buttery, rich character.

» FEW AMERICAN BARREL-AGED GIN
46.5% | Chicago, USA

Another small-batch gin, this one from a tiny distillery in Chicago. Unlike most distilleries, which employ a neutral tasting spirit for the heart of their gin, FEW uses a rich grain spirit that it produces itself, creating a London Dry gin that is then aged in both new American oak and "used" American oak. Batches are around 120 bottles only, giving hints of orange, lemon, thyme, and crucially, juniper.

» FOUR PILLARS RARE DRY GIN
41.8% | Australia

First the Aussie whisky boom, and now comes a gin one! The latest leading the charge is Four Pillars, who base everything they do on – you've guessed it – four pillars: their copper still, Wilma; water from the Yarra Valley; local botanicals including pepper berry leaf and lemon myrtle; and a whole lotta love from the team of distillers. Brilliantly bonzer stuff, guys.

» NO.3 LONDON DRY GIN
46% | Holland

Paying homage to the spiritual home of gin in Holland, No.3 London Dry Gin is all about simplicity and tradition, being specially formulated for London's oldest wine merchants, Berry Bros & Rudd of No.3 St James's Street, Mayfair. Predominantly juniper-heavy with strong cardamom notes and a hint of lemon peel, it is gloriously simplistic and hefty, making it ideal for luxurious Martinis. An absolute classic in our eyes.

VODKA

The Perfect Mixer

SPIRIT NAME	ETYMOLOGY/COUNTRY OF ORIGIN	COLOUR	MAIN COUNTRIES OF PRODUCTION	BIGGEST-SELLING GLOBAL BRANDS	KEY INGREDIENTS
Vodka. Polish: *wódka*; Russian: *водка*.	Both Russia and Poland lay claim to the origins of vodka production in the eighth or ninth century.	Crystal clear.	The "Vodka Belt", covering Russia, Ukraine, Belarus, the Nordics, and Poland, but can often include northern Germany and some other Eastern European states. Plus the USA and UK, where leading brand Smirnoff is produced.	Smirnoff, Absolut, Belenkaya, Pyat Ozer, Krupnik, and Grey Goose.	Traditional vodka must be made from potatoes, cereals, or molasses. The "Vodka Wars" and subsequent Schnellhardt Compromise means that vodka made from any other ingredient must state as such on the label (*see* pp.56–7).

VODKA

The Perfect Mixer

When it comes to distilled drinks, many people's first experience is with vodka. The perfect mixer, vodka is often used simply to give standard drinks a little more kick. A measure of vodka in your cola, apple juice, or ginger ale is the ground floor on the elevator to discovering the skyscraper of spirits.

A simple spirit, good vodka has many uses, from easy mixability to a straight shot or even a slow-sipping number. It can be flavoured or infused and distilled once, twice, or multiples thereof, and as a result, is probably the most malleable spirit in the whole of the distilled-drinks portfolio.

Originating in Eastern Europe and now distilled the world over, vodka is the ideal additive to many a cocktail, and this is reflected in its global sales. Flanked by the foot soldiers that are flavoured spirits such as gin and infused vodkas, vodka is ready to ride into battle, fearless of no one, to conquer the drinks realm from its headquarters in Eastern Europe. As brands go, the flag-waving leader of the pack is Smirnoff. Selling over 24 million cases a year globally, it is the second biggest-selling spirits brand in the world.

PURITY VERSUS PERSONALITY

Vodka's detractors tend to be found in the world of dark spirits – those matured for a period of time or the distilled drinks that carry a weight of flavour to them. But why does such a ubiquitously consumed spirit get so much flak within the drinks business? The simple answer to this comes in the form of one word: purity.

In its simplest form, vodka is pure distilled spirit. Over the years it has become fashionable to distil vodka to the highest-possible level of purity, and this is often viewed by drinks experts as resulting in a lack of flavour

and personality. In fact, it is this purity, or absence of impurity, that gives vodka its strength (versatility) but also its weakness (lack of strong flavour).

However, with the dawn of the ultra-pure spirit carrying the name vodka comes creative refinements from smaller producers. These "added extras" include using water to cut the spirit down and an increased focus on the base product from which the vodka is produced. These innovations have brought brands such as Cîroc into play (*see* p.56–7), which trumpets its production from grapes and five-times distillation.

This has opened up a whole new field in the vodka segment,

> *It is this purity, or absence of impurity, that gives vodka its strength (versatility) but also its weakness (lack of strong flavour).*

enabling certain brands to occupy the higher end of the pricing scale and offer ultra-premium editions previously unseen in the straightforward world of vodka.

And as much as "purity" can be marketed as a positive, the more a spirit is distilled, rectified, and purified, the more it is being stripped of flavour and personality. So here in this book, we are looking for brands and distilled liquids that express both personality and narrative by the bottle-load.

SIMPLY DISTILLING

Vodka is one of the most simply made of all the spirits you can purchase today. Unlike single malt Scotch whisky, which is produced by distilling a beer made exclusively from malted barley, or Tequila, made from the blue agave plant, vodka is a distillation of a brew using any available agricultural product. This could be anything from wheat or other grains to potatoes – or even cheese (*see* p.65). Once distilled, it is bottled as a pure, white spirit and not matured. One could argue, then, that any unmatured, highly purified spirit can be called vodka, but therein lies the key to what vodka really is: pure spirit.

This pure spirit is created by extracting starches and sugars that can be fermented into alcohol. With potatoes, this is done in the same way as with

← Vodka shots are often people's first experience with a spirit.
↑ Clean, crisp, pure: modern top-notch vodka is made in sophisticated and well-designed environments.

grains in other fermentation processes: by washing out the huge amount of starch hidden inside each spud. Anyone who has overboiled potatoes will know how the water turns out – murky and misty. This isn't a good result when cooking them, but is exactly what you want if you are going to make vodka.

Once the potatoes have been rinsed of their starch and the fermentation process kicked off, all that is left to do is to distil, purifying the vodka to the desired levels – either utterly clean and crisp or leaving some of the flavours of the base ingredient behind.

On the Trail of Vodka's Lineage

With some spirits it is relatively simple to trace their origins. Scotch from Scotland, Caribbean rum, or Portuguese port – many spirits are rooted deep in the fabric of a nation, while others have a clearly defined discovery point.

For centuries, vodka has been seen as the purest of all spirits, but the origins and historical significance of this globally consumed drink are considerably cloudier. While its precise provenance remains enigmatic, at the same time vodka is hugely symbolic in the development of many great Eastern European states throughout the last several hundred years. Vodka has been the fuel of much mythology, formed the centrepiece of political conflict, and served to loosen tongues in countless espionage chronicles the world over.

Today, the global vodka market is larger than any other spirit, accounting for around 20 per cent of all spirits sold.

It would be an exhaustive process to detail the history of the spirit from a worldwide perspective, so instead we shall look specifically at production in what has widely become known as the "Vodka Belt" – an area running across the agricultural countries that lie to the northeast of Europe and extend into Scandinavia.

WHAT THE VODKA WARS REVEALED

The battle over the lineage of vodka proper has been played out in the courtrooms of the European Union on two notable occasions in recent times, which nicely illustrate the key issues of the spirit's evolution over centuries past.

The first of these vodka wars was over who had the right to claim the country of origin for the spirit. Things came to a head in the late 1970s when the Soviet Union and Poland waged a battle over the exclusive rights to label their brands with the word "vodka", both sides citing many historical texts alluding to its origins. The conflict ended in a draw, with both sides producing convincing evidence but no conclusive ruling being made.

It was nearly two decades later, after a European Commission proposal to bring in different categories of vodka, that the "Vodka Belt" community joined forces to argue that only a spirit made from potatoes, cereal, or molasses could be called vodka.

What caused this rumpus was the launch of a new "vodka" brand called Cîroc, which uses grapes as its base product, giving a sweeter and smoother flavour profile in stark contrast to the traditions of the spirit.

In the early days of vodka production in the eighth to ninth centuries, distillation often led to a rough, impure spirit unpleasant to the nose, let alone

← All eyes on this man: a Polish potato farmer.
↑ New styles of vodka – often flavoured – and new brands are appearing all the time, such as the highly successful Cîroc from France.

the taste-buds. To compensate for these undesirable attributes, flavourings such as an infusion of herbs were often added to the spirits to make them more palatable as medicinal tinctures.

By the end of the sixteenth century, vodka had become a widely consumed beverage across Eastern Europe, with differing grains and potatoes being used according to available harvests. While it is now commonplace for some brands of vodka to use a single grain in production, back then a multitude of base ingredients were used to make quality vodka. Traditionally, potatoes and sugar beet produced a cheap, fermentable mash seen as inferior to that using more expensive wheat or rye.

And this is where Cîroc caused such a stir. The "Vodka Belt" countries believed that this spirit, made as it was from grapes, shouldn't carry the same moniker as their products, as it was not distilled from grain, molasses, or potatoes. With other vodka-producing countries wanting a broader definition of the spirit, it was the German politician Horst Schnellhardt who devised a compromise: namely that spirit produced from anything other than potatoes, cereal, and molasses should be labelled as "Vodka made from…"

The Schnellhardt Compromise now helps consumers around the world to identify the lineage of their chosen vodka spirit and, most importantly, imparts empowering knowledge to the most important person in the vodka chain: you.

VODKA'S

Cocktail Contribution

Cocktails are all about flavour. If you have never made one before, don't worry. Just find a few tasty, non-alcoholic liquid ingredients and add some complementary alcoholic liquid to it. A punch is the very best example of this.

Punch

Many cocktails, especially those served in a coupe or Martini glass, are often held up as objects to admire, works of art to be placed on a pedestal and viewed with some reverence. Punch, on the other hand, is a campfire of a cocktail – it is to be huddled around, fuelling conversation and acting as the very best social glue.

A punch is also a really useful way to give your spirits cabinet a bit of a clean-out. Undoubtedly, there will be some bottles hanging around at the back of your cabinet that have either been purchased in haste or received as a rather misguided gift from friends. All of these items can be used in a punch to pretty simple effect, so long as you have the key ingredient ready: vodka.

The backbone of any good punch, vodka will give it the alcoholic kick that it needs and will also act as the sticking plaster across the various flavours of fruit juices and booze that have been lovingly* combined to create your very own bespoke lubricant for the evening.

The rules of a good punch are pretty simple:

✳ Get a good base down with whatever spirits you have left in your cupboard.
✳ Add fruit juice, ice, and slices of orange, apple, strawberries, or whatever is in season, sampling as you go. If in doubt, add more ice and fruit juice.
✳ Add vodka.
✳ If it's cold outdoors, make sure that you heat up your punch.

And there you have it: a tasty alcoholic complex.

or simply thrown together

THE CLASSIC DUO

The Mule & the Martini

Vodka has been the foundation of many classic cocktails. In the gin section of this book, we look at the Martini (*see* p.40), favoured by us using gin but perfectly acceptable with vodka too (*see* opposite, left). In the book and the movie *Casino Royale*, Ian Fleming's James Bond creates his own bastard version of the two by using both gin and vodka (remarking to his bartender after he's just made it that the drink would be better with a grain-based vodka), given the title "Vesper" after a female character who appears later in the proceedings. His measures are three of gin (Gordon's is the choice made), one of vodka, and a half-measure of Kina Lillet (probably the best wine-based apéritif around, to add some sweetness). A killer combo of three alcohols to kick-start any adventure for a member of the British Secret Service.

The Mule (*see* opposite, left) is a cocktail that centres on the use of ginger beer as a key ingredient. Of the mule family, the Moscow Mule is probably the most famous, and, as you can guess from the name, is a mix of ginger beer, two shots of vodka, and fresh lime served over ice in a tall glass. Simple and easy and especially welcome on a hot summer's day, this cocktail is a good introduction to the world of vodka.

Meet the Maverick

» DAN AYKROYD
CRYSTAL HEAD VODKA, NEWFOUNDLAND, CANADA
....

From ghostbuster to spirit producer, Canadian acting royalty Dan Aykroyd launched his very own vodka brand back in 2008 (*see* p.65) with a truly captivating bottle design, based on the legend of the Mayan–Aztec crystal skulls. But as Dan reveals, the liquid is every bit as magical...

How did the whole Crystal Head project come about?
"My experience as a spirits manufacturer began on a blustery winter's night at my friend, artist John Alexander's, loft. We were talking about wines, Tequilas, rums, vodkas, and their respective vessels. The Frangelico bottle [shaped like a monk's body with a little white cord around it] has always been a favourite of ours. When John suggested a skull bottle, my response was positive, but I didn't think he could produce a design within two minutes of proposing it to me! His Mayan–Aztec–Navajo-inspired head has sold in excess of two million bottles."

So would you describe yourself as a connoisseur of vodka, or an enthusiast?
"I am an enthusiast. However, we have all learned a lot about how lesser vodkas are made. Crystal Head is quality certified – we stripped out the traditional additives from the beverage. How could we put the usual junk – glycol, citrus oil, and raw sugar – into our sacredly inspired vessel?"

So what would be the perfect Dan Aykroyd Crystal Head cocktail? You strike us as a Martini drinker.
"I actually love sipping Crystal Head straight from a frozen shot glass. Also, we've been enjoying it straight up as a chilled Virgin Martini in a rocks glass."

Here's a tough one for you. Creator of an exquisite, quality spirit or a ghostbuster. Which of these would you rather be remembered as?
"I will be remembered longer for being a ghostbuster, but Crystal Head will be a popular exquisite product much longer than the eventual final output of the *Ghostbusters* franchise."

Describe your current state of mind in three words.
"Ink. Molecules. Paper."

10

VODKAS TO TRY

Vodka is an interesting spirit, often distilled to the point of no (flavour) return. Along with bottled water, it can probably be considered as one of the best examples of marketing a product. However, not all vodka is the same and here we look not just at the great marketing stories (vodka from cheese, anyone?) but at the flavours inside the bottles too.

» CHASE SMOKED ENGLISH OAK VODKA
40% | Herefordshire, England

Having sold the Tyrrells brand of crisps, the family behind Chase developed a distillery on their farm to put to good use the overflow of potatoes that was a legacy of potato-chip production. William Chase focuses on classic clean, crisp, potato-based vodka. This smoked edition is enhanced by delicate smoke from English oak, giving a flavour more akin to a mezcal (*see* pp.74–5) than a vodka.

» POTOCKI VODKA
40% | Poland

The history and heritage of this vodka requires no massaging from a marketing person. With original documents verifying production dating back to 1784, it has one of the strongest histories in distillation. The spirit today is made from rye, twice-distilled at the Polmos Łańcut distillery and lightly filtered before bottling to retain its strength of flavour and classic earthy finish. A must-try for quality, consistency, and history alone.

» CRYSTAL HEAD VODKA
40% | Canada

One of the most eye-catching bottle designs ever to be produced, not just in vodka but the spirits world in general, Crystal Head has been developed in part by comedy legend Dan Aykroyd (see pp.62–3). With the bottle made by Bruni Glass in Italy, the spirit inside is quadruple-distilled and then filtered through double-terminated quartz crystals, also known as Herkimer diamonds. Hints of minerals add depth to this pure vodka.

» REYKA VODKA
40% | Iceland

The first distillery to make vodka in Iceland, Reyka produces small batches of 890 litres (195 gallons) at a time from wheat and barley in a traditional (and rare) copper Carter-Head-style still. The distillery in Borgarnes, on the southwestern tip of Iceland, was built in 2005 by William Grant & Sons, a Scottish-owned company famous for making whisky. Here the vodka is filtered through local lava rock before bottling. The spirit is floral and light, with hints of vanilla.

» BLACK COW PURE MILK VODKA
40% | Dorset, England

Dorset cheese-maker (yes, cheese-maker) Jason Barber makes award-winning cheese. In order to do so, he takes milk from his local cows and separates it into curds and whey. The curd goes off to become cheese. And his whey? Using a special yeast, he creates a milk beer that is then distilled into vodka, of course! The spirit is creamy and sweet, with a warming quality. Mooo-ve over, Russia! Here comes an English cow farmer.

» VESTAL KASZEBE VODKA
40% | Poland

Set up in Poland by father-and-son team John and William Borrell, the former with a history in the wine industry, Vestal focuses on both vintages and terroir (the natural environment), illustrating how different potato types from different fields and grown under varying conditions affect flavour. The Kaszebe edition is distilled from the Vineta potato grown in the region from which the vodka takes its name. A grain edition is also available.

» SIPSMITH BARLEY VODKA
40% | London, England

Sipsmith set up its small West London operation in 2009, joining the likes of Beefeater to become one of the very few copper pot still operations in the city (see p.20) – the first in nearly two centuries, in fact. The barley vodka is highly acclaimed: distilled using the 300-litre (66-gallon) still named Prudence, it is cut down to bottling strength using water from one of the source springs of the River Thames. With a spiced, nutty nature, this is an English rose of a vodka.

» GREY GOOSE VODKA
40% | Picardy, France

When the idea of employing the knowledge of the folk who have made Cognac for hundreds of years was married with that of using premium French winter wheat – for which the country's baked products are so famous, and which is ideal for making vodka – Grey Goose was born. A spirit produced in northern France, yet with a heart and soul in the Cognac region, it is fruity and delicious.

» PUR VODKA
40% | Quebec, Canada

Despite its proximity to Russia, Canada is more famed for maple syrup and Arcade Fire than it is for vodka. However, after a boom in craft brewing, there is a small but vibrant scene of micro-distilleries popping up, alongside the more famous and larger whisky distilleries. The producer of PUR vodka uses water from a source north of the city that has been filtered through the local granite rock. A crisp vodka that sits well on the palate, this really is worth seeking out.

» PURITY VODKA
40% | Sweden

Perhaps more famous for Absolut, Sweden produces a number of vodkas, with Purity often lauded as one of the best – not just in Sweden but in the world. Made at Ellinge Castle Distillery in the south of Sweden, Purity Vodka is distilled 34 times through a still made from copper and gold. It is produced from wheat and barley and then put together by Master Blender Thomas Kuuttanen. Smooth, with an oily palate and a mineral-rich flavour, this is worth exploring.

TEQUILA

Head of the Versatile Agave Family

SPIRIT NAME	ETYMOLOGY/ COUNTRY OF ORIGIN	COLOUR	MAIN COUNTRIES OF PRODUCTION	BIGGEST-SELLING GLOBAL BRANDS	KEY INGREDIENTS
Tequila. The name is derived from the Mexican town of Tequila, which lies to the northwest of the major city of Guadalajara.	Mexico. Although an agave spirit may have been produced by the Aztecs at an earlier date, records show that Spanish conquistadors were distilling the first form of Tequila using the agave plant in the mid-sixteenth century.	Tequila can range from clear, unaged spirit – *blanco* – to light gold – *reposado*, or "rested" – and a vibrant gold – *añejo*, or "aged". Some Tequilas are extra-*añejo*, giving an even richer golden hue.	Mexico. There are five Mexican states that are legally allowed to produce Tequila: Jalisco and parts of Guanajuato, Tamaulipas, Michoacán, and Nayarit.	Jose Cuervo, Olmeca, Sauza, Cabo Wabo, Don Julio, Patron, Pepe Lopez, and Herradura.	The agave plant (a succulent native to Mexico) is first cooked to help release the juice, which is then fermented and distilled in copper or stainless-steel stills. Some Tequilas (*reposado* and *añejo*) are then aged in oak casks.

TEQUILA

Head of the Versatile Agave Family

One Tequila, two Tequila, three Tequila… floor!

Please excuse the above sloganeering, which is often seen on a particularly faded, ill-fitting T-shirt worn by a person who really should know better than to discuss their drinking habits openly in public through the medium of leisurewear. But as you are already (many) pages into this book, we don't feel bad about making the following confession: until recently, Tequila was "the drink that cannot be named" for both of us. By this we mean that nearly every adult, at some stage of their lives, has overindulged in a particular spirit, whereby afterwards, sometimes for decades, even the merest whiff sets the pulse racing and the stomach churning. But learning from your mistakes and discovering a more educated and intelligent side to spirits is what this book is all about, and fortunately, a few years ago we had the good fortune to meet a gentleman bartender who completely cured us of our past transgressions with this iconic Mexican spirit. What we learned was that doors are for slamming, not Tequila.

← *A gentle ageing process in oak casks is hugely important for both reposado and añejo-style Tequilas.*
↘ *Cutting the piñas: preparing the hearts of the agave plants before cooking, fermenting and then distilling them.*

of guests: a preserved agave worm (actually a caterpillar) or, even worse, some other multi-legged creature usually found scurrying around a plantation. Apart from rendering a spirit undrinkable (although to be honest, the additional protein might add a modicum of flavour to these insipid creations), the image we are left with is one of a sad, neglected drink that is only let out of the box when there is nothing else drinkable at a party.

But, thankfully, times they are a-changin' – and fast. Both Tequila and mezcal have undergone a fantastic reboot over the last few years and the age-old craftsmanship that has been passed like a bottle of the good stuff between generations is finally making its way from the remotest farms of Mexico to the shelves of the most premium spirits retailers in the world.

THE *GRAND CRU* OF AGAVES

From grape to grain and fruit to vegetable, practically every spirit-producing nation relies on what grows in abundance – and for Mexico, the agave plant or *maguey*, with its more-than-

TIME FOR A REAPPRAISAL

Tequila is a wonderfully versatile drink. Its silky, fragrant layers work as perfectly when sipped from a tasting glass as when mixed into a savoury Bloody Maria cocktail. But in some ways, the spirit has been unfairly shackled to the notion that it is little more than a warming, pungent shot that buddies well with a slice of lime and a line of salt. Not in these pages, sunshine, not in these pages.

Mezcal is the misunderstood brother of Tequila (we'll delve into their relationship later on – *see* pp.74–5) in that when given the chance to shine, it offers as much variety and vitality as some of the most diversely flavoured single malt whiskies in the world. In some ways, mezcal has fared even worse than Tequila, with a bottle of mezcal becoming the classic gift from a friend returning home after a holiday to Mexico, many including that most unwanted passing resemblance to both cacti and the aloe, is the lifeblood and essential base ingredient for making Tequila and mezcal.

But what do we know about this sensational succulent? Well, for a start, to dispel a common misconception, it isn't related to the cactus, despite the similar ominous-looking spiny leaves and protrusions, but exists in a unique genus of its own. There are over 200 recorded varieties of agave, but for the production of Tequila, the blue agave stands out, and by law this is the only variety permitted in the production of Tequila.

Blue agave is the *grand cru* of agaves, and the juice (*aguamiel*, or "honey water") is highly prized by distillers. The variety is native to the main Tequila-producing region of Jalisco and is favoured because of its naturally high proportion of sugars, which are perfect for turning into alcohol during distillation. But the distillers have to pay more than just a high price for the best examples of this essential building block of premium Tequila. In fact, they need to keep themselves busy for at least 10–12 years until the plant has reached full maturity. Then and only then can the *jimadores*, the Mexican farmers who harvest these prize beasts, begin their painstaking work.

GETTING TO THE HEART OF THE MATTER

The history of Mexican agave spirits can be traced back to the sixteenth century, but the agave plant itself has a symbolic, ritualistic heritage dating from earlier times and was woven into the Aztec way of life of over a thousand years ago. As the plant has a high moisture content, the Aztecs extracted the sweet sap from inside its heart and fermented it, producing a cloudy, slightly sour-tasting alcoholic drink known as *pulque*. It was the hallowed beverage at the scene of religious festivals and sacrifices, where high priests would celebrate Mayahuel, the goddess of the *maguey*, believing the plant's sweet nectar to be the deity's lifeblood.

When Spanish conquistadors settled in Mexico in 1521, they bought with them a huge supply of brandy. But as this ran out, they used their knowledge of distillation to turn *pulque* into a spirit, and the very first agave distillate – initially crude and harsh tasting – was born. The conquistadors refined the process by turning directly to the agave plant. They cooked the hearts, or *piñas* (so named because of their resemblance to a pineapple), slowly over fires, which broke down heavy starches and allowed the natural sweetness to develop. The hearts were then crushed, naturally fermented, and distilled, often in simple ceramic stills.

The name Tequila comes from the town of Tequila near Guadalajara in the state of Jalisco, where the volcanic landscape was rich with the precious blue agave plants, and it is now a protected industry, much in the same way as Cognac or Calvados. As its popularity grew, enduring brands came to life and both the Sauza and Cuervo marques (Cuervo built the first licensed distillery in 1758) were among the first to export their spirits outside of Mexico.

COMMERCIAL VERSUS TRADITIONAL PRODUCTION

....

Today, production of Tequila is a modern, streamlined process for most large companies, which have dispensed with the more traditional ways. In fact, a large number of mass-market Tequilas are not produced from 100 per cent blue agave and are known as *mixtos*, where a minimum 51 per cent agave content is supplemented by other sugar sources before the spirit is distilled, producing a Tequila that is not only less authentic but unflattering on the palate. However, smaller distillers still firmly adhere to the rustic and time-consuming methods to obtain the very best results.

The agave *piñas* are still hand-harvested and prepared before being transferred to steam-heated ovens to cook slowly for up to four days in order to soften the fleshy hearts. By way of an example, the average *piña* weighs in at a hefty 60–70kg (132–154lb) and it takes about 7kg (15½lb) of agave to produce just 1 litre (1¾ pints) of 100 per cent pure Tequila.

Hugely commercial ventures have turned the process into a much shorter, less labour-intensive enterprise, with vast steam pressure cookers taking the place of the more traditional stone ovens. They will produce quicker results (sometimes around six hours' cooking time), but many artisanal producers believe that extracting the

precious sugars takes time and by rushing the process an element of bitterness can enter the *mosto*, or predistilled fermented agave liquid, which in turn produces an inferior-tasting Tequila.

The softened *piñas* are then ground by rollers and shredded before being placed in large, open fermentation vats. A more traditional method uses a huge, stone-carved *tahona* wheel, which was once pulled by a mule to slowly compact the agave into a pulp. Yeast and a little water are added to the vats and the agave *mosto*, and after several days of fermentation (the length of time, between three and 10 days, all depends on the temperature and weather conditions), the liquid that is drained off is usually around 5%

ABV. It is then distilled twice (with some companies distilling a third time) in either copper pot stills or, on a larger scale, more efficient column-style stills (*see* pp.20–1), and a clear spirit of around 40% ABV is collected.

At this point the spirit really enters an entire realm of its own. Unlike new-make whisky spirit, which unquestionably has its particular character, fresh Tequila spirit doesn't need to be legally aged, and the key for any distiller is to retain as much of the natural agave flavour as possible to deliver a well-rounded and unique spirit. Distilling it many times for the sake of purity just removes valuable traces of flavour.

TEQUILA STYLES AND SUBSTANCE

Blanco Tequilas are bottled at this stage to retain their fresh, clean character profile, while *reposado* and *añejo* styles are aged in oak casks – predominantly ex-American bourbon and French oak casks, which round out the flavours, delivering colour as well as additional flavours from the type of wood used. *Reposados* are merely "rested" in cask for a minimum of two months and up to one year, often to give them just a quick tickle of additional flavour (rather like giving a tea bag a quick dunk), whereas *añejos* have a minimum of one year's ageing, often being left to mature for up to three years.

The key for any distiller is to retain as much of the natural agave flavour as possible to deliver a well-rounded and unique spirit.

← A traditional tahona *wheel, used to crush the cooked and softened agave.*
↑ *Tequila bottles showing off the region in which they were produced.*

Extra-*añejos* are matured for three years upwards and the wood type starts to have a profound effect on the overall flavour, with heavy, spiced notes mixing with vanilla, drying oaky tones, and sometimes port- or wine-influenced flavours.

It is hugely subjective, but while the extra-*añejo* Tequilas offer a broader flavour profile and are more appealing to drinkers of other dark spirits, such as whisky, Cognac, Armagnac, or rum, they begin to lose their naked appeal: the crisp, peppery, almost savoury note that pure agave delivers on the palate. But happily, this also makes Tequila an enormously versatile spirit with a multitude of uses and serves (*see* pp.80–1 for our most enjoyable suggestions).

MEZCAL

Tequila's Reserved Yet Rewarding Hermano

There's no hiding from the huge international popularity of Tequila. Visit any bar practically anywhere in the world and there, on the back, will be a bottle waiting to serenade you with its distinctly Mexican charm. Tequila is the glamorous, urbane, party-loving spirit, up until the small hours with a *joie de vivre* and a spring in its stack-heeled step.

Mezcal, on the other hand, is a very different personality altogether. Rustic and traditional, it is not as culturally aware as its stylish *hermano* (brother), but has huge hidden depths, once you get to know it. It may prefer a night in at home with a good book, but when the conversation starts flowing, you will be transfixed by what's on offer.

↑ *Three "rustic" examples of mezcal displayed for sale.*

So why has mezcal been overshadowed by Tequila? Technically speaking, Tequila is a type of mezcal and its production methods are rooted in the same traditions, which date back to the sixteenth century. In the same way that some French brandy became recognized as Cognac and Armagnac, Tequila has a number of specifically designated production areas that were defined in Mexican law in 1994, with the most prolific centred around Guadalajara in the Jalisco region towards the north. Mezcal production is concentrated much further south, around the state of Oaxaca. Both use agave as their base ingredient (*see* p.78 for a more detailed description of the agaves used in mezcal production), but in terms of flavour, it is mezcal that arguably has a much broader and complex flavour profile. Yet for decades it has sat in the shadows, waiting to be discovered.

Part of this travesty has been the aforementioned stigma with "that worm" (*see* p.80 for how the worm has well and truly turned). Whereas Tequila tapped into both the social and, over the last two decades, the connoisseur side of the spirit, mezcal was seen as a thuggish alternative: crude, harsh, and poorly made, with the worm signifying that a bottle of this stuff has a "potency" about it. It was there for the conquest, a mouthful of worm at the end to show that you had gone the distance with this bruiser.

Then, a little over 20 years ago, the truth was revealed. Deep in the farmland around Oaxaca – an area that is now designated as the key mezcal-producing region in Mexico and home to over 90 per cent of the mezcal distilleries – the true quality of this deeply spiritual product became apparent and, thankfully, the rustic settings, traditional production techniques, and centuries of skill are now being shared with the rest of the world.

Meet the Maverick

» **RON COOPER**
DEL MAGUEY MEZCAL, SANTA FE, USA

A highly successful artist, Ron is also the founder of Del Maguey Mezcal (meaning "from the plant"), which has located, bottled, and distributed artisanal mezcals from tiny single village distilleries around Oaxaca in Mexico since 1995. Ron is a fount of knowledge when it comes to the agave plant and is the undisputed godfather of the ever-expanding international popularity of mezcal. Sir, we salute you.

When did you first discover mezcal?

"Well, there's a Mexican *dichos* (phrase) that you don't find mezcal, it finds you, and I definitely got 'found'. I guess it was back in 1963, when I was in art school and I took a trip with friends to a bar in Baja California. I got drunk as hell on an agave spirit and never looked back. In 1970, I had an art exhibition on with a few friends and we were drinking Herradura Blanco, the best Tequila in the 1970s. The conversation got round to travelling down the mythical Pan-American Highway to Panama. Two weeks later we were off, with surfboards on the roof of our van, and four months later we arrived in Panama, but on the way we discovered Oaxaca in Mexico, the home of mezcal. In due course it became my headquarters, and the more time I spent there, I discovered the ritual use of the spirit."

So how did you find the best distilleries? They must have been completely untapped outside of Oaxaca.

"I used to return to California with plastic containers and sometimes gas cans full of amazing mezcal! In 1990, I spent three months travelling down the dirt roads in a truck, stopping locals and asking *'Donde es el mejor?'* ('Where's the best?') I found 28 amazing samples this way, as well as participating in an eight-day-long Zapotec wedding, where they gave me a five-gallon jar of Chichicapa mezcal in exchange for smuggling someone across the border! The border guards made me pour most of it away, but I managed to rescue some, and at that moment I vowed no one would ever stop me from bringing mezcal into the US."

How difficult was it to convince all these villages you represent that you were the real deal and not just there to rip them off?

"Hell, *I* wasn't even convinced! I was seen as an alien when I arrived to negotiate with them – kids used to run away when they saw my truck arriving! But a few fearless producers saw the opportunity and I bottled my first mezcals in 1995: Chichicapa and San Luis Del Rio. We have around 10 producers now, one, which takes about 12 hours to visit, down a rocky dirt road. Slowly I began to bring these producers together. Now they're a group formally recognized by the Mexican government."

How many types of agave do you use to produce mezcal?

"Well, it's generally accepted that there are about 30 different varieties of agave, although each agave has three different names for different producers! Some of them can take as long as 25–30 years to mature. One of the rarest, the wild *tobala* agave, only grows in some of the highest-altitude environments in the shade of oak trees, like the truffle."

Does Mezcal age at all?

"Ninety-nine per cent of our mezcals are put straight into the bottle without ageing. However, when I started, I used to put them in stainless-steel beer barrels. After a while I noticed that they had started to change: mature, and mellow out a little. The flavour softened, which I suspect is down to oxidization. I have only a few bottles left of the very first mezcal I ever bottled – a 1995 from a small distillery in Chichicapa (a small town two hours' drive south of Oaxaca); I probably bottled too many and didn't sell it straight away. The distiller came by and when he tried a bottle (which had been in storage) his draw dropped! He hadn't been able to hang on to anything for longer than six months, so the bottle-ageing had really made a difference to the flavour."

Describe Del Maguey in three words.

"True agave mother."

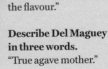

5

Indipensable Tequila & Mezcal Facts

* Tequila is a form of agave-based spirit, much in the same way that mezcal is. The main difference is that Tequila has to be made from the *Agave tequilana* Weber Blue or the blue agave plant, whereas mezcal can be made from a wider variety of agave species.

* Unaged Tequila is known as a *blanco* or sometimes as silver Tequila. Aged Tequila (*reposado* or *añejo*) is often filled into ex-American bourbon barrels, French wine casks, or, to obtain a greater wood influence, new-oak casks that have been charred on the inside.

* Mezcal often takes on a distinct smoky aroma and flavour profile because of the traditional process of heating the agave hearts for a long time in deep earth and stone-filled pits, which are covered by wood and the discarded spiny, fibrous leaves from the agave plant.

* The world's most expensive Tequila, Ultra Premium Tequila Ley .925 Pasión Azteca to give it its full name, costs a heady (and frankly absurd) $225,000 (about £136,000) a bottle.

* Continuing with the bling, Mexican scientists have pioneered a way to create real diamonds by super-heating Tequila to 800°C/1,472°F. You won't be able to wear them, though – the precious stones are so small that their application is only really useful for creating microchips and extra-fine cutting instruments.

MEZCAL AND THE MEXICAN TERROIR

Because of the more liberal use of different species of agave in mezcal, the spirit has developed a much more distinct set of flavours than Tequila. As a result, mezcal perhaps embodies the spirit of terroir like no other spirit.

A GENTLE SMOKINESS

Some connoisseurs compare mezcal to the whiskies produced on the Isle of Islay in the Inner Hebrides in Scotland, which have a pronounced smokiness to them – some more so than others, such as Laphroaig or Lagavulin. In fact, mezcal develops its smoky flavour and aroma from the initial preparation of the agave *piñas*. Rather than cook them in steam-heated ovens, farmers dig deep pits that are then lined with firewood and stones, on which the *piñas* are slowly roasted for over eight hours. Once the fires have died down, the pits are covered with the discarded fibrous leaves from the agave plants, tarpaulins, and mountains of earth, and the *piñas* sit, slowly infusing with the oily, smoky residue of the ashes and coals for up to five days. The smoke influence makes its way into the bottle and you will find some mezcals that have just a faint wisp of smoke, with others offering a much heavier, bonfire note on the nose and palate.

← Many smaller mezcal producers still rely on tried-and-tested methods during distillation. If it ain't broke...

mean that certain agave types have become highly adept at survival. Agave plants, including the commonly used *espadín* (or "sword" variety) and *tepestate* are generally harvested after around five to six years, but certain strains, such as the wild *tobala* grow erratically in more challenging soil conditions (often on mountain terraces), so require longer to mature.

The agaves open their pores up at night and absorb moisture from the atmosphere, closing up tightly in the daytime to stop releasing any valuable succulence. But in mezcal production, *maguey* plants are deliberately not harvested during the monsoon season in Oaxaca, between June and August. According to Ron Cooper, founder of Del Maguey Mezcal (*see* pp.76–7), "Ground water forces its way up into the roots, making the plants bitter, so you would end up with a poor spirit. We always wait until September/October to harvest, to allow the plants to dry out."

WILD FERMENTATION

Most artisanal, small-batch mezcals are fermented using the wild yeasts that naturally occur in the air surrounding the distilleries, and it is these strains that help to influence the overall character of the resulting spirit, due to how effective they are at turning all the lovely sweet, sugary juices from the agave into alcohol. Traditional mezcals are fermented in the open air, sometimes for as long as 14–30 days.

AGAVE TYPE

Like grape varieties, different agaves will add a fundamental distinction to the flavour of a mezcal. Because of the mountainous nature of the undulating Mexican landscape, the soil type and hot conditions

THE WORM HAS (THANKFULLY) TURNED

"It took me about 18 years to kill that f***ing worm," laughs Ron Cooper, founder of Del Maguey Mezcal (*see* pp.76–7), "but finally it is long forgotten."

Ron continues: "The story goes that in the 1940s, an art student, who was working at a liquor store in Texas, started to make a little money on the side by recycling glass bottles and selling them on. He thought that if he filled them with something cheap, he could make even more money, so he went to Oaxaca to locate the cheapest mezcal available. What he found was spirit made from agave plants that had been harvested after their peak, which were rotting and infested with grubs – not worms at all but the larvae of the night moth. After coming up with the clever [if slightly unpleasant] idea of adding a worm to each bottle, the brand Gusano Rojo ['red worm'] Mezcal was born, as one of the first commercially available mezcals in the US."

Today, the jolly image of the worm still gazes out from the bottle, looking a little like a wriggly Michelin Man. The urban myth is that eating the worm will produce all manner of hallucinogenic effects, but you are more likely just to get a horrendous hangover from having consumed too much of the spirit rather than have anything that resembles an out-of-body experience.

HOW TO ENJOY TEQUILA & MEZCAL

OK, there is an element to this section of the book that we don't want to sound all preachy. Enjoying Tequila is above all probably one of the easiest things to do, so this may come across a little like sucking agave-flavoured eggs, but in that context, let's take a step back from the happy-go-lucky image of the spirit.

When sipped and savoured in the right kind of glass, Tequila

⌐ *Forget slamming. The complex flavours found in 100% agave Tequila deserve your undivided attention.*

can be as beguiling as any dark spirit, delivering complexity as well as a range of unique flavours from bottle to bottle and from style to style. When it comes to mezcal, the same thing applies and much more...

"No one should shoot mezcal like some macho idiot to get drunk," thinks Ron Cooper. In fact, mezcal shares so many similar traits with the complex flavours of Islay whisky that allowing the spirit to breathe in a nosing glass or wine glass really brings out the gentle smokiness against a wonderful backdrop of fresh fruits and darker earthy spices. Above all else, take your time.

But this section really wouldn't feel complete without a counterpoint to the more reserved and perhaps sensible approach to appreciating both spirits. Let's not forget that one of the most enduring cocktails of all time, the Margarita, needs the uniqueness of Tequila for it to be a success. Here's our guide to probably the very best example of this undisputed classic, alongside a mezcal serve.

Sotol

SHH, IT'S MEXICO'S SECRET SPIRIT

High in the north of Mexico, not far from its border with the USA, is the city of Chihuahua, which is the spiritual home to Mexico's third national spirit, sotol. This rarely seen spirit is produced in very similar ways to Tequila and mezcal but uses the *Dasylirion wheeleri*, or desert spoon plant, another succulent shrub-like agave, as its base ingredient. As there are so few commercial producers of this spirit, it is doubtful that you will find a bottle in any but the best, well-stocked spirits retailers (*see* p.87 for details of perhaps the most likely example), but if you do, it's well worth investigating, as it has a much more herb-driven, almost root-like spiciness to it.

TOMMY'S

Margarita

This drink has been named after Tommy's, a very famous Mexican restaurant in San Francisco, USA, where this simple but stupendous version of the classic Margarita was first conceived. Made with *reposado* 100 per cent agave Tequila and fresh ingredients, this is perhaps the perfect way to reintroduce someone to the world of Tequila. The key is the balance of natural sweetness from the agave syrup, the citric burst from a fresh lime, and the clean-yet-wonderfully rounded profile of the *reposado* Tequila, which delivers additional sweetness and notes of vanilla.

INGREDIENTS

50ml (2 measures) *reposado* Tequila
our suggestion would be Herradura Reposado

❊

25ml (1 measure) fresh lime juice

❊

12ml (½ measure) agave syrup
Thankfully, this is much easier to get hold of now in a variety of supermarkets and health-food shops; it's super-sweet but supposedly much healthier than other syrups, though we're not sure we'd want to put it on our porridge in the morning.

METHOD

Add everything to a cocktail shaker with fresh ice. Shake like crazy and strain into a Margarita coupe glass or, for a twist, over ice in a tumbler. Garnish with a slice of lime.

✳

Oaxaca Old Fashioned

Again, swap out the base of a classic drink for a truly unique and distinctly Mexican tinge. The smokiness in the mezcal adds an uncommonly good dimension to an Old Fashioned and pairs nicely with the rich sweetness and zesty orange.

INGREDIENTS

50ml (2 measures) Del Maguey Vida Single Village Mezcal *(see* p.86*)*

✳

12ml (½ measure) brown sugar syrup, or a brown sugar cube

✳

3 dashes Angostura bitters

✳

freshly pared orange and lemon zests

METHOD

Build your drink slowly by stirring the ingredients in a large rocks glass, adding ice as the cocktail becomes diluted. Anything less than five minutes' preparation (especially if you are breaking down a sugar cube) is not even trying.

10
TEQUILAS & MEZCALS
(Plus a Sotol)
TO TRY

Although both of these incredible spirits are effectively cut from the same cloth (the remarkable agave plant), they remain unique when it comes to flavour. So here are our picks for an array of highly interesting Tequilas you may not have tried, alongside a handful of exceptionally well-made mezcals – and a sotol thrown in for good measure. *Salud*!

» DEL MAGUEY PECHUGA SINGLE VILLAGE MEZCAL
49% | Oaxaca, Mexico

Pechuga is a triple-distilled mezcal whose final distillation involves, unusually, a basket of fruit, spice, and a whole chicken breast. The spirit vapours pass through this wholesome hamper of delights and the result is a wonderfully fruity, meaty flavour, alongside the clean, serene, vegetative notes of mezcal. A true delicacy and one of the most sought-after bottlings of mezcal in the world.

» ILEGAL MEZCAL JOVEN
40% | Guatemala (via Oaxaca!), Mexico

Back in 2004, John Rexer began to import (smuggle) the best mezcals he could find from Oaxaca to stock his bar, Café No Sé, in La Antigua, Guatemala. One bottle became five, which became 10, and before he knew it, John had all manner of people illicitly bringing him spirit. In 2009, his operation went legit. This mezcal has notes of medicinal smoke, peppercorns and cooked root vegetables, alongside toffee/popcorn sweetness.

» FORTALEZA AÑEJO TEQUILA
40% | Jalisco, Mexico

As histories go, Fortaleza can trace its roots back over five generations and 140 years of making fine tequila. This wonderfully rich, buttery sweet Añejo has been matured in American oak casks for up to 18 months, and double distilled in copper pots, using agave that has been stone crushed and fermented in open air wooden tanks.

» OCHO BLANCO TEQUILA
40% | Jalisco, Mexico

Another superb bottling from the sensational Carlos Camarena, in partnership with agave expert, Tomas Estes, this silver tequila possesses a deliciously clean palate, with notes of fresh limes, some sweeter vegetative notes and a very distinct freshness, followed by a sprinkling of white pepper. Ocho is about as versatile as Tequila can be; it makes a delectable Bloody Maria and yet is smooth enough to sip as a palate-cleanser. Top marks.

» HACIENDA DE CHIHUAHUA SOTOL AÑEJO
38% | Chihuahua, Mexico

Hacienda de Chihuahua is probably the best-known producer of sotol, another member of the Mexican spirit family (*see* box, p.81). Made from the desert spoon plant, which takes as long as 15 years to mature, sotol possesses a more spicy, herbaceous note than Tequila. This example is aged for six months in French wine casks, giving earthy, root-laden flavours of liquorice, lemon grass, and dried fruit.

» GRAN CENTENARIO ROSANGEL TEQUILA
40% | Hacienda Los Camichines, Jalisco, Mexico

Purists may wince at this addition, but who cares when you have something this tasty in your glass? Rosangel is an infused *reposado* Tequila, which starts with 10 months' maturation in French wine casks and is then rested for two months in old port barrels, helping to develop its sweet orchard fruit notes, and then infused with hibiscus flowers.

» AQUARIVA REPOSADO BAR TEQUILA
38% | Los Altos, Jalisco, Mexico

Cleo Rocos, actress and sidekick to the late British comedian Kenny Everett, has become a highly respected authority on Tequila, and AquaRiva is the result of years of development to produce a high-quality 100-per-cent blue agave Tequila that both sips well and mixes perfectly. Aged in bourbon casks for a minimum of three years, there are notes of fresh fruit, acacia honey, and oaty biscuits.

» PATRON SILVER TEQUILA
40% | Jalisco, Mexico

One of the most well-known 100% agave tequilas in the world, this fabulously clean spirit justifies its place on this hallowed list thanks to the hugely herbaceous/ peppery notes that you'll taste on the first sip, coupled with the fact that the Hacienda where it is distilled is one of the most intriguing places to visit, if you're interested in the production of tequila. If you find yourself in Guadalajara, make sure you give them a call.

» DEL MAGUEY VIDA SINGLE VILLAGE MEZCAL
42% | Oaxaca, Mexico

Without wanting to favour Del Maguey too heavily, we had to include this outstanding mezcal alongside its more exclusive sibling Pechuga (*see* top left) as an outright affordable introduction to this unique spirit. For anyone beginning their journey into mezcal, Vida has everything: subtle smokiness, black pepper, a burst of fresh fruit, and a distinct medicinal note that conjures up an Islay Scotch whisky.

» LOS DANZANTES AÑEJO MEZCAL
45.4% | Santiago Matatlán, Oaxaca, Mexico

Meaning "the dancers", Los Danzantes is a series of successful restaurants in southern Mexico, founded by Gustavo Muñoz, who then turned distiller, building a small artisanal operation back in 1997. The distillery offers a rare sight – *reposado* and *añejo* mezcals matured in oak casks from Limousin in France. This *añejo* has a rich honeycomb note coupled with soft smoke, a hint of fresh bananas, and then a robust, oaky spice.

ABSINTHE

The Magical Green Fairy

SPIRIT NAME	ETYMOLOGY/ COUNTRY OF ORIGIN	COLOUR	MAIN COUNTRIES OF PRODUCTION	BIGGEST-SELLING GLOBAL BRANDS	KEY INGREDIENTS
Absinthe. Derived from the Latin name for grand wormwood, *Artemisia absinthium*.	First produced in Switzerland back in the 1790s, then popularized across the border in France.	Traditionally, French-made absinthe has taken a slight jade hue, ranging to a vibrant bright green. Swiss absinthes are historically clear.	France, Switzerland, Czech Republic, and, since 2007, the USA.	La Fée, Pernod, and Lucid.	Neutral spirit (traditionally grape-based) is redistilled or sometimes infused with green aniseed (also called anise), fennel, and, most importantly, grand wormwood (*see* left), along with a host of other botanicals.

ABSINTHE

The Magical Green Fairy

As you have chosen to pick up this book, which is essentially all about spirits, we are fairly sure that you are acutely aware of the effects alcohol has on the mind and body. But two to three thousand years ago, maybe the same reference points didn't really apply.

In the gin section of this book, we mentioned the destructive nature of the gin craze back in the eighteenth century and how a once-celebrated drink was swiftly reviled and virtually driven out of town because of its heady, intoxicating effects on the masses (*see* p.38). But while London had "Madam Geneva" to contend with, over in France, the authorities were preparing themselves for battle against an even more potent foe: *la fée verte* or "the green fairy" herself, absinthe.

Absinthe is one of those spirits that very few drinkers have ventured towards without an element of precaution. With its notoriously high ABV of around an eye-watering 70%, its bitter, herbaceous flavour, and supposed hallucinogenic properties, absinthe is never going to take the place of a nice, easy-drinking rum or whisky, or be as mixer-friendly as gin or vodka (ironic, given gin's murky past), but that's what makes it such an exciting proposition. No matter what scrapes certain spirits have got themselves into in the past, absinthe has managed to go one step further in the notoriety stakes, and for a long time it was outlawed in a number of countries. Consider it the *Clockwork Orange* of the spirit world.

But with all its insalubrious association, historically absinthe has a much more celebrated association. It was at the heart of the Belle Époque era and it will forever be connected with numerous luminaries from the literary and artistic world. So why did absinthe become such an *enfant terrible*?

Artemisia Absinthium

AWAY WITH THE GREEN FAIRY
....

At the centre of absinthe lies *Artemisia absinthium*, or grand wormwood, a remarkable plant which, since ancient Greek times, has been celebrated for its medicinal properties.

Distilled wormwood followed this medicinal route back in the late eighteenth century, when Pierre Ordinaire, a French doctor living in the Couvet area of Switzerland, created a cure-all tonic containing the herb. It proved popular and the recipe made its way into the hands of a commercial distiller, who began to distil larger quantities of the spirit. The absinthe produced in Switzerland won a reputation, and a further distillery was then built across the French border in Pontarlier (which has since become the spiritual home of absinthe), run by Henry-Louis Pernod, when the spirit under the brand name Pernod Fils gained its potent foothold.

Absinthe was entering its heyday, with its reputed medicinal properties helping soldiers in Algeria to ward off malaria. Parisian cafés and bars also bought into the simple yet potent nature of the spirit. In fact, if you were a noted dandy in the mid- to late 1800s, it's likely that at around 5pm every day you would assemble with your suitably well-dressed friends in a café for *l'heure verte* ("the green hour") to savour a glass of absinthe. On the table next to you, you would perhaps catch a glimpse of Edouard Manet, Toulouse-Lautrec, and Van Gogh gazing into their green-tinged glasses

Absinthe was seen by acolytes of the Belle Époque era of France as a means of expanding their minds and creativity.

← *Wormwood – the bitter (supposedly hallucinogenic) heart of absinthe.*
↓*A typical perforated absinthe spoon – essential for the traditional way of serving this potent spirit (see p.101).*

for inspiration. Similarly, at the back of the café, Arthur Rimbaud, Paul Verlaine, and Oscar Wilde would be penning missives and poems in homage to *la fée verte*. In fact, Wilde once said that the after-effects of drinking absinthe were much like the feeling of having tulips on his legs.

So why did the drink become such a hit with these bohemian artists and celebrated minds? Well, here's where absinthe enters another dimension altogether when compared to its contemporaries. Wormwood is noted for containing the chemical compound called thujone, which purportedly carries with it mind-altering qualities and psychoactive effects. By way of example, head back to 1895 and the painting *La Muse Verte* by Albert Maignan. The miraculous, hallucinogenic imagery conjured up on the canvas articulately highlights a poet succumbing to the effects of the green fairy. Absinthe (and its reported after-effects) was seen by many artists, writers, and other acolytes of the Belle Époque era of France as a means of expanding their minds and creativity. The LSD of its day? Perhaps. But to throw in a little science for a second, for any real hallucinatory effects to take place, a drinker would have to have consumed so much absinthe that they would either be stone dead from alcohol poisoning or at the very least completely unconscious!

BAD FAIRY

In the late 1800s, absinthe sales went through the roof, thanks in part to a persistent little pest called the phylloxera bug, which took a shine to the grape vines relied upon by the French wine and Cognac business. With their wares in extremely short supply, prices went up and absinthe was a readily available alternative for drinkers across France. But its days were numbered. Its extraordinarily high strength began to take its toll on society, leading to increased crime, drunkenness, and unrest, and temperance movements of the time called for it to be banned.

The curious case of "the absinthe murders" sank the final nail into the coffin of the spirit. A certain Swiss farmer killed his entire family while under the influence of alcohol, and absinthe squarely took the blame – despite the fact that he had consumed vast quantities of wine and crème de menthe before finishing with just one glass of the green stuff.

In a few years, absinthe was banned in Switzerland, France, the USA, and the Netherlands. But contrary to popular belief, it was never banned in the UK; instead, interest in the spirit waned due to a lack of availability. Poorly produced versions of absinthe surfaced in the 1990s, but these bore no real resemblance to the quality distillates of the past, most being artificially flavoured high-strength spirits.

↗ Absinthe-minded: Van Gogh was said to have been a big fan of the notorious spirit.

GOOD FAIRY

Fortunately though, through a network of collectors, enthusiasts, and disciples, absinthe clawed its way back onto the shelves and the legal bans were lifted at the turn of the millennium, with original absinthe distilleries in Pontarlier harking back to long-lost recipes. Recently, brand-new craft distilleries have begun

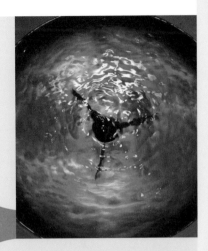

to re-establish an artisanal theme when it comes to making absinthe, producing exceptional small-batch examples from locally sourced wormwood and other botanicals.

Coupled with a firm interest in classic cocktails and vintage paraphernalia, suddenly the absinthe fairy is gracefully floating around again, weaving her magic on yet another generation of believers.

WHAT MAKES THE FAIRY GREEN?

The production of absinthe has a number of similarities to gin in that a neutral spirit, largely a very high-strength (70% plus ABV) grape-based eau-de-vie, is redistilled with the essential flavours, which include fennel and green aniseed, as well as the all-important wormwood. Major commercial absinthes are often artificially coloured green before being bottled. However, a number of higher-end, quality absinthes are made, with a proportion of the botanicals being steeped in alcohol, which brings a more vibrant natural green colouring that the spirit is famous for. In fact, leave a bottle of quality absinthe in direct sunlight (please don't actually do this) and you will notice a distinct change in colour as the natural chlorophyll reacts with the sunlight.

PASTIS & ARAK

The Aromatic Aniseed Relations

With aniseed having such a unique flavour, it is little wonder that many other spirits alongside absinthe have also laid a claim to this flavoursome spice, notably pastis and arak.

PASTIS – IT'S NOT A PASTICHE

When absinthe was eventually banned in France back in 1915, French distillers looked to capitalize on the vacuum left by the spirit. They realized that by removing the wormwood (which was deemed the offending botanical in absinthe) and considerably lowering the alcohol strength to around 40–45% ABV, they could still market a great-tasting spirit, with aniseed and liquorice root being the central players. Born in the early 1930s, pastis had all of the familiar flavours associated with absinthe but with no repercussions. Brands like Pernod and Paul Ricard remain successful today, with a huge domestic following. Pastis is enjoyed in the same way as absinthe – served diluted, it is then "louched" with water (*see* p.101), giving the glass a cloudy, milky appearance.

ARAK – LEBANESE DELIGHT WITH A BITE

Known for its colourful history of winemaking, Lebanon has also popularized a potent and flavoursome drink called arak. Similar to pastis, this clear, aniseed-flavoured liqueur is usually bottled at around 59% ABV. Arak has a number of cousins across the Eastern Mediterranean in the shape of raki in Turkey and ouzo in Greece, and they are all essentially derived from the same methods, sometimes using sugar, dates, or figs as the base ingredient for the spirit

↑ Ricard is one of the best known brands of pastis around the world.

and redistilled or additionally flavoured with aniseed.

Lebanese arak is made from the grapes of the last harvests, which are left to ferment in barrels for several weeks and the resulting mixture is then distilled several times and mixed with a small quantity of aniseed flavouring.

Arak is traditionally drunk at mealtimes with mezze-style dishes and mixes well with spiced lamb dishes such as makanek or kibbe. Over in Iraq, arak is just as popular and is often referred to as "lion's milk" because of its cloudy appearance and high alcoholic content, only tolerated by drinkers "as strong as lions".

Meet the Maverick

» **JOSEPH PAWELSKI**
OVERLAND DISTILLERY, COLORADO, USA

From his base in Loveland, Colorado,
Joseph Pawelski has turned his attention
to making a traditional absinthe, but
with strictly American wormwood.

What's the ethos behind your distillery?
"Overland Distillery is committed to bringing back spirits, flavours, and culture that have been lost to time. Our products contain only naturally grown ingredients, and most of those ingredients are cultivated and hand-harvested on arms we've established here in Colorado. We believe that what's in the bottle matters."

What makes your absinthe unique?
"Trinity Absinthe is built upon several historic absinthe recipes, yet is characterized by a slight variation of spice and a smoothness not commonly found in most other absinthe brands [*see* pp.104–5]. This makes Trinity Absinthe a great brand to use both in the traditional manner, with ice-cold water, as well as in cocktails. We only use organic ingredients and our leaf herbs are naturally grown and hand-harvested, then carefully dried right here in northern Colorado. This is the only way we have found to get the quality and flavours we demand."

Have you been influenced by the location of the distillery, from a flavour perspective?
"The combination of high elevation and a dry, sunny climate lends itself well to growing most absinthe herbs. Like wine grapes, absinthe herbs take on some of the flavours of

the region in which they are grown. Our experience is that Colorado herbs tend to be more aromatic and our wormwood tastes sweeter and is more floral than the wormwood we've sampled from Pontarlier and other common absinthe production regions. As far as we know, we are the first formally to grow wormwood and other absinthe herbs in Colorado at any scale, so it was a bit of an experiment at first. We were quite happy and somewhat surprised when our herbs turned out so well!"

As a craft distiller, what keeps your passion ticking over?
"Ingenuity. There are many things, both good and bad, that have been made exactly the same for generations. Ingenuity in craft distilling uses the good

aspects of old traditions as a foundation, yet takes liberties in transforming lesser aspects into the best aspects, often producing new and delicious creations along the way."

What lessons have you learned as a craft distiller?
"My passions are distilling and making things. Becoming a craft distiller requires skill in business, accounting, marketing, a lot of patience, some amount of starting cash, and, most of all, persistence."

What are your plans for the future?
"I'd love to see absinthe become the bar staple it once was. Of course, if the staple absinthe is Trinity Absinthe, all the better! But like gin and whiskey, the more the merrier!"

HOW TO ENJOY ABSINTHE

One reason that absinthe has managed to traverse leaner times is the traditional preparation of the drink, which positively borders on the ritualistic. With its customary high strength (absinthes were historically bottled almost immediately after distillation, with around 60–75% ABV, a tradition that continues today), the flavours really needed releasing from their spirity grasp. So the absinthe would be prepared meticulously with a 3:1 ratio of water to spirit.

THE SINNING SERVE

Haven't I seen someone setting absinthe alight, you ask? Well, you may have, but they jolly well need their lighter confiscating. Igniting an absinthe-coated sugar cube, which melts into the glass to create a flaming drink, bears no resemblance to the traditional "French Method" of preparing absinthe (*see* opposite). In fact, "The Bohemian Method" was developed in the Czech Republic, partly to disguise the appalling taste of poorly made absinthes available in the 1990s.

→ *The water-drip fountain. This traditional way to serve absinthe, diluted by drops of chilled water, makes the classic "slow pour" of Guinness seem positively hasty!*

THE TRADITIONAL SERVE

Ice water would be dripped slowly onto a small cube of cane sugar, held in place on a specifically shaped perforated silver spoon (*see* photo, p.93), to sweeten the preparation. As the water reacts with the essential oils of the wormwood, fennel, and aniseed, a cloudy "louching" effect takes place, giving the appearance of a mist emerging from within the glass.

THE "HOLY GRAIL" OF SERVES

As the popularity of absinthe grew in the early 1900s, so did the fascination with the "perfect" serve, with distilleries, bars, and cafés going to tremendous lengths to give their absinthe devotees the best imbibing experience, with incredibly ornately designed spoons to dissolve the sugar upon, and perhaps most striking of all, the absinthe fountain (*see* opposite), often a four-person dispenser that effortlessly dripped iced water through little taps into the waiting glasses (which were of course purpose-designed). Today, the fascination for the "absinthe experience" has seen bars locating antique fountains and spoons, which resemble museum pieces but perfectly illustrate the theatre of the spirit. As a result, absinthe is the quintessential "take your time" spirit. There is no hurrying the green fairy.

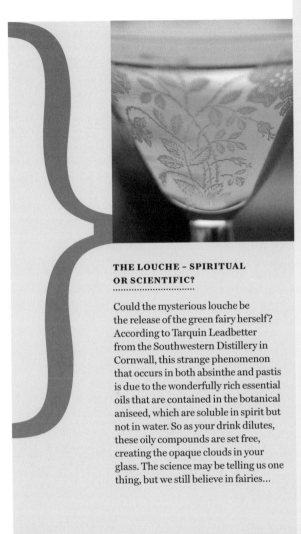

THE LOUCHE – SPIRITUAL OR SCIENTIFIC?

Could the mysterious louche be the release of the green fairy herself? According to Tarquin Leadbetter from the Southwestern Distillery in Cornwall, this strange phenomenon that occurs in both absinthe and pastis is due to the wonderfully rich essential oils that are contained in the botanical aniseed, which are soluble in spirit but not in water. So as your drink dilutes, these oily compounds are set free, creating the opaque clouds in your glass. The science may be telling us one thing, but we still believe in fairies...

*

Corpse Reviver No.2

Because absinthe has such a highly developed and powerful flavour profile, with aniseed, fennel, and bitter wormwood at its heart, it is a tough beast to mix in a cocktail, especially as a main ingredient. But used sparingly, as a "wash" for one's cocktail glass, or in minute quantities, it can bring incredible complexity to a number of classic cocktails, none more so than the fabulously named Corpse Reviver No.2, first popularized by the great Harry Craddock, bartender at the Savoy Hotel, London, in the 1920s.

INGREDIENTS

20ml (¾ measure) London Dry gin. Beefeater original works very well

*

20ml (¾ measure) Cointreau

*

20ml (¾ measure) Lillet Blanc, a wonderfully citrus-filled fortified wine

*

20ml (¾ measure) freshly squeezed lemon juice

*

10ml (scant ⅓ measure) absinthe

*

twist of lemon zest, to garnish

METHOD

Add all the ingredients to a shaker with ice and shake like crazy until you are on the verge of seeing fairies just through dizziness alone. Strain into a chilled Martini glass and garnish with a twist of lemon zest. Has the medicinal power to stop a rhino-sized hangover dead in its tracks, and the absinthe gives the drink a subtle but cleansing herbaceous note.

» 10

ABSINTHES & PASTIS TO TRY

With its legendary potency, absinthe is a tough choice for a drink to be sipped and savoured. But in our opinion the following (despite their undoubted high strengths) demonstrate the many wonderful subtleties you can find in a well-made spirit with a unique recipe.

» PERNOD ABSINTHE
68% | Thuir, France

Dating back to 1805, the Pernod Fils distillery, built by Henri-Louis Pernod, produced what is widely believed to be the first commercial absinthe. But the stills fell silent after absinthe's extended period in the sin bin and it would take another 200 years for Pernod to recreate the original recipe, building a new distillery in Thuir. This newly released absinthe has a distinct aniseed note on the nose, with a mildly herbal bitterness on the palate.

» ABSINTHE ROQUETTE 1797
75% | Pontarlier, France

A beast of an absinthe, Roquette is complex, unusual, and spicy. Based directly on a late eighteenth-century recipe, from when the drink straddled the line between liquor and potion, it has a faint green tinge and is slow to louche (*see* p.101), retaining some clarity. Full of vegetative, almost parsnip notes, cumin, and a bitter wormwood note. Take your time with this and you'll be transported back to the heart of the Belle Epoque.

» ADNAMS ROUGE ABSINTHE
66% | Southwold, Suffolk, England

Distilled in the gleaming copper house at the Adnams Distillery, Southwold, this absinthe eschews the traditions of chasing the green fairy in favour of a much more vibrant, smouldering red colour. Its distinctive tinge comes from hibiscus flowers, which also lend a subtle floral note to the nose, alongside notes of fennel, dry spice, and coriander. Gentlemen of Southwold, for daring to be different, we salute you!

» SOUTHWESTERN DISTILLERY PASTIS
42% | Cornwall, England

We couldn't resist this: a Cornish pastis. Tarquin Leadbetter's tiny West Country distillery has created a true first – the only pastis to be distilled outside of France – and crafts it in batches of just 300 bottles at a time. Tarquin forages gorse flowers (that give a sweet coconut note) from local clifftops and distills them with more traditional herbaceous botanicals, including aniseed and fresh orange zest.

» OVERLAND TRINITY ABSINTHE
63% | Colorado, USA

When the Pawelskis established their distillery in 2009, they struck gold (well, green, we suppose) by discovering that the local landscape of Loveland contained an abundance of wormwood (*see* pp.98–9). Trinity brings together this locally sourced ingredient with fennel and aniseed (the other two players in this triumvirate of herbal flavour) to give a very traditional dry and highly aromatic absinthe that casts a wonderful louche (*see* p.101) with ice water.

» LA MAISON FONTAINE ABSINTHE
56% | Pontarlier, France

This clear absinthe is lovingly put together at the Émile Pernot distillery, with a mix of around 15 botanicals and a strong presence of a particular vegetative fennel note. What struck us most here, though, was how wonderfully crisp and zesty this absinthe is – well worth trying with a decent tonic water (*see* pp.42–3) for a refreshingly different take on how to enjoy the spirit.

» LA CLANDESTINE ABSINTHE
53% | Couvet, Switzerland

An absinthe made at the birthplace of the spirit, in the Val-de-Travers region of Switzerland. Clear and quick to louche (*see* p.101), it has a distinct minty flavour, a dusty, savoury note and a clean fennel aroma. It is a lot sweeter than other absinthes and requires minimal sugar. The palate bursts with aniseed, a peppery piquancy lingering in the mouth for a long time. If French isn't your fancy, then look no further.

» LA FÉE XS ABSINTHE SUISSE
53% | Switzerland

This is the flagship of the most popular brand of absinthe since the spirit was reintroduced to a new audience at the turn of the millennium. Rather like La Clandestine (*see* left), it is crystal-clear and has a very quick louche (*see* p.101), with lots of dry, medicinal notes emerging first, followed by more familiar aniseed. It is a less intense experience than some of the French absinthes, developing an almost creamy note on the palate.

» ABSINTHE SAUVAGE 1804
68% | Pontarlier, France

When absinthe fanatic David Nathan-Maister went in search of the best wormwood in France, little did he know he would be scrambling up mountain paths with a local farmer to find wild crops of this aromatic gem. Sauvage (meaning "wild") is unlike any absinthe we have ever encountered, with powerful bitter notes balancing herbaceous fennel and a complex palate of spices. If absinthe had a *grand cru*, this would be it.

» HENRI BARDOUIN PASTIS
45% | Forcalquier, France

Unique and explosive on the palate, this has over 50 different botanicals vying for your attention! Despite being proudly French, Henri Bardouin Pastis has not followed the pack with a powerful star anise note (a different flavour to the green aniseed used in absinthe), but balances cardamom, angelica, rosemary, liquorice, and thyme with more unusual botanicals such as sweet woodruff, lemon verbena, and tonka bean.

RUM

The Pirate Spirit of the Caribbean

SPIRIT NAME	ETYMOLOGY/ COUNTRY OF ORIGIN	COLOUR	MAIN COUNTRIES OF PRODUCTION	BIGGEST-SELLING GLOBAL BRANDS	KEY INGREDIENTS
Rum, rhum, rhum agricole, cachaça. "Brazilian rum" is used as an alternative name to cachaça.	Cuba and other Caribbean Islands and Latin America.	Clear when bottled directly from the stills. Dark or "golden" when matured in oak casks.	Cuba and other Caribbean Islands, Latin America, India, and Australia. Cachaça in Brazil only and rhum agricole in Martinique.	Bacardi, Tanduay, McDowell's, Captain Morgan, Brugal, Havana Club, Contessa, and Cacique.	Sugar-cane products such as molasses or fresh sugar-cane juice.

→ *La Bodeguita del Medio in Havana. Imitated worldwide, but arguably never bettered...*

RUM

The Pirate Spirit of the Caribbean

Rum is less of a drink and more of a way of life. Sweet and eminently quaffable, rum has established itself as a classic drink on its own or in cocktails, and the history of the drink has a story as rich as the flavours found in most bottles.

The majority of rum is produced in the Caribbean and Latin America, evoking scenes of Johnny Depp dressed as a pirate and hightailing it around the deck of a ship, but the product is not exclusive to these areas and is made the world over, from India to Spain. With historical links to sugar-cane farming, rum production can even be found on small, less-well-known islands such as the volcanic Réunion to the east of Madagascar, and it is these islands that produce some of the most unusual offerings found in the Rum market today.

THE SAILOR'S TOT

Rum's association with pirates and buccaneers is no fable and the drink's link with the navy is even stronger, with it having been the traditional liquor of choice for seamen in the British Navy, issued as a daily ration of "grog" to keep them going on the high seas.

This naval ration was known as a "tot" and the practice of pouring and drinking known as "totting". It was still commonplace in the navy until 1970, when it was finally abolished by the British government. However, totting does still happen aboard Royal Navy ships, but now only on the specific orders of either the Queen (or her appointee) or a senior member of the Royal Navy, who will announce "splice the main brace" to signal that a drink should be shared. This expression comes from the reward – a tot – for the men who carried out difficult emergency repair jobs on sailing ships, and has remained to this day as the call to reward a difficult job well done.

The sailors in the Royal Navy didn't exactly welcome the removal of the daily rum ration from their diets, and dubbed the fateful date, July 31, 1970, "Black Tot Day". It's a date now often marked by rum producers with

← *Port out, rum home: sailors would queue up for their daily tot of rum, a practice outlawed only in 1970.*

events or releases, and there is even a rum brand shrewdly called Black Tot.

It's not just the tot or the catchphrase "splice the main brace" that provide the link between the navy and rum; its very own style, "Navy Strength" rum, is what also binds the spirit to sailors. The monikers "Navy" rum, "Navy Strength" rum, or "Naval" rum have no set definition, but today these labels generally refer to the style of rum that would have been found on board naval ships from the 1600s through to the infamous Black Tot Day in 1970. During those hundred or so years, navy rum moved from the bridge to the bottle, with famous brands such as Lamb's and Smith & Cross hitting the shelves and paying homage to the sailor's choice, which tends to have a richer flavour as well as being bottled at a higher strength.

LIFESAVING LIQUOR

These two key factors of pronounced flavour and high strength were not just marketing gimmicks but had a vital and potentially lifesaving role. The enhanced flavour was due in part to the rum being stored in casks and taking on the greater depth and complexity that extra maturation in wood brings. But this increase in flavour also allowed for the rum to be mixed with lime juice, an important dietary supplement for the sailors in warding off scurvy.

The higher proof of these naval rums also helped to prolong the life span of the liquor on-board ship; barrel-aged spirit experiences a drop in ABV over time, so on a long journey across the oceans, starting with a high-strength alcohol made sense.

The second major factor in favour of taking high-strength rum on board was safety. Long before the days of the health-and-safety officer, it was considered a positive that a high-strength alcoholic spirit was also a big fire risk. As with the origin of the "proof" system (*see* p.219) whereby the strength of a spirit was measured ("proved") in terms of its combustibility when mixed with gunpowder and set alight, the same attribute was required on a warship. If you are away on a mission to stop pirates on the high seas, or to escort trade ships through dangerous waters, you really need your gunpowder to do its thing. And if you are carrying low-alcohol-strength rum that leaks, diluting your gunpowder, then that's exactly what will happen: no cannon, no defence, and the very real threat of an attack by hordes of mermaids. Perish the thought.

So, for the sailors of the British Navy, the most successful maritime force of their age, rum was a saviour, keeping them sane in their squalid living conditions, warding off all sorts of diseases from the drinking of stale water, and, unlike beer, without stopping them from using their vital weapons when they needed to.

Choose Your Favourite Shade of Rum

As tasty as Navy Strength rum is, it's not the only version of this sweet liquor. Rum has many different versions, often graded according to colour.

WHITE OR LIGHT RUM

This is unaged rum, or at least rum that hasn't sat for a long time in a cask, often drawn and bottled directly from the still. Best used in cocktails.

GOLDEN RUM

A halfway point between the white rums and the dark rums, golden rum is aged for a short period of time, giving some colour and flavour influence from the oak casks.

DARK RUM

The "finest" of the rums, these have been aged for an extra-long time in oak casks, often ones that have first been used for Cognac, whiskey, or bourbon. This variety is especially good for sipping. Be careful, however, as rum can be post-coloured with caramel colouring or molasses additives.

SPICED RUM

Delicious as the ever-increasingly dark rums may be, one of the most well-known versions is spiced rum. Produced by adding different flavours such as cinnamon, vanilla, and orange peel, it can come in white, golden, or, most commonly, dark form. Again, the older, aged versions are great for drinking neat, with the younger, lighter versions perfect for cocktails.

ISLANDS OF INFLUENCE

The trade routes of the Atlantic Ocean have played a major part in the seeding of rum from individual islands to the rest of the world. Not only did the transportation by sea allow for rum to mature in casks, mellowing the spirit sufficiently to take on a golden hue and round off the harshness of the raw distillate into a smoother, more developed and concentrated flavour, it also allowed the spirit to become the ultimate source of cash and credit in the colonial balance of payments. Rum became a major commodity traded in exchange for slaves on the African coast, lending a darker side to its history, now long-since resigned to the past in its transformation into a light-hearted party drink.

Although it is the smaller Caribbean islands such as Antigua, Barbados, and the Bahamas that can lay claim to be the originators of the first widely produced rums, it was the island of Cuba that launched many of the famous brands we know today, such as Havana Club and Bacardi.

One of the world's most recognized spirit brands, Havana Club currently has a split personality, depending on where you are in the world. Globally, Havana Club is a joint venture between Pernod Ricard and the Cuban government, selling rum made, as the name would suggest, in Cuba.

← Rum is very much a pouring drink used in a wide variety of popular cocktails, although aged versions can be sipped slowly by connoisseurs.

what is effectively a beer. In fact, the origins of whisky pay homage to the "preservation" of beer through distillation. In rum production, the sugar-cane "wine" can also be consumed neat, and in the Philippines this is highly regarded as a drink in its own right, known as *basi*.

But back to our production of rum... Producing a spirit is like ordering a pizza: first you choose your base (in the case of rum, that's sugar) and then you choose your toppings (the method of distillation). You have your classic style (pizza margherita), which is pot still distillation (*see* p.20), or you have something more "modern" (BBQ chicken pizza, if you like), which is column still distillation (*see* p.21). Like vodka, rum is a 50/50 pizza: there are no hard-and-fast rules as to which method of distillation should be used. Some rums are produced in a classic pot still way while others are run through column stills.

Once the spirit has been captured from the distillation, it can be bottled pure as a white rum, matured in oak casks as a dark or golden rum, and even flavoured as a spiced rum (*see* opposite). Whichever way, it can then be labelled with those three important letters – R-U-M.

However, due to an historical diffusion of the brand, the ownership in the USA is highly contested. Coupled with the embargo on Cuban products in the States, the rum available under the Havana Club label in the USA is actually produced by Bacardi in Puerto Rico. This rum is available only in small quantities, predominantly in the state of Florida.

Rum, in both its white and golden forms, has established itself as an essential back-bar bottle. Whether it is consumed neat or in cocktails, it has become one of the world's largest spirit categories, with no sign of shying away from the resurgent success it has seen over the last decade.

PRODUCTION VALUES

As you would expect from a product so heavily linked with the Caribbean and other islands, rum is made from a variety of sugars or sugar derivatives such as molasses following our now-familiar road of fermentation and distillation.

In other spirit products – malt whisky, for instance – an additional process is needed to help break down the starches in the base product into sugars, which can then be processed by yeast to create alcohol. Yet with rum we are already dealing with sugar, so the yeast can go straight to work in producing alcohol.

With a grain-based spirit, the fermentation stage produces

RHUM AGRICOLE & CACHAÇA

The Charismatic Sugar Cane Cousins

RHUM AGRICOLE

Rhum agricole is produced in a slightly different way to rum, using freshly squeezed sugar-cane juice as opposed to molasses, with the French island of Martinique having its own controlled appellation under European Union law, where juice can only be taken from sugar cane grown in 23 designated regions of the island.

Martinique rhum agricole comes in three varieties:

❖ *Blanc*
This variety is colourless and under three months of age.
❖ *Élevé sous bois*
Denoting rhum agricoles that have been aged for a minimum of 12 months.
❖ *Vieux*
Older rhum agricoles that are laid down for at least three years.

It should be noted, however, that rhum agricole can be made anywhere, and is often found in production at other standard rum distilleries, but only those produced from local sugar-cane juice in Martinique follow the above rules.

CACHAÇA

Made in a similar way to rhum agricole, cachaça is the equivalent Brazilian sugar-cane spirit. Until the middle of 2013, when a new law was passed, one of cachaça's main markets, the USA, called all cane-sugar spirit "rum". Cachaça fell outside the global legal definition of rum because *some* cachaças use accelerants, such as malted barley, in the fermentation stage, and were therefore labelled "Brazilian rum" in the States. However, after much lobbying from both the cachaça producers

and the Brazilian government, the law was finally changed to allow bottles that had been produced in Brazil to carry the term "cachaça", leaving off the moniker "Brazilian rum". Nowadays, cachaça is by some distance the most popular spirit in Brazil (helped by high import taxes on foreign spirits).

Early cachaça production has its foundations in the sugar-cane plantations that the Portuguese developed in Brazil during the sixteenth century. Already skilled distillers, the Portuguese found that, without too much bother, a sweet, tasty spirit could

be created from the fermented juice of the sugar cane.

Like rum, cachaça takes two forms: unaged (white) and aged (gold). Cachaça is most famous outside of Brazil for being part of the Caipirinha cocktail (*see* p.116), which we feel is *the* way to consume this sweet product.

→ *This vintage rum advert bears testament to the spirit's appeal through the ages.*

RUM-BASED COCKTAIL CLASSICS

The Caipirinha

Those who read novels will often tell you that when a book is turned into a film it is never quite as good as the original. Given a Hollywood sheen, glamorous actors, and a more palatable approach, the whole thing is designed for greater mass appeal, and most of the time it works, with blockbusters born from bestsellers. The Caipirinha is, for us, the original book to the million-selling, sweet-and-approachable Mojito movie. The latter, a classic white rum-based cocktail, is similar in construction to the Brazilian Caipirinha, but watered down with soda, mellowed with mint, and sweetened with oodles of sugar. The Caipirinha, on the other hand, is the straight-up version, as follows.

METHOD

Grab a handful of lime wedges, throw them into an Old Fashioned glass, and, using a muddler, crush them to release the juice. Pour in 50ml (2 measures) of cachaça, a small teaspoonful of sugar syrup, and ice (crushed or cubed), then give it a good old stir. Stick in a straw and, Bob's-your-uncle (or Davi's-your-dad for the Brazilians), you have an ultra-refreshing, strong, and delicious cocktail that's perfect on a hot summer's day.

✳
—

The Hurricane

If you happen to have a spirits cupboard overflowing with bottles of various rums and you fancy using them up in something other than a punch (*see* our punch advice on p.58), then a good place to start is with the Hurricane cocktail, so famous that, like the Old Fashioned, it even has a glass named after it.

Essentially, the Hurricane is both white and dark rum mixed together with a tropical fruit juice, such as lime, pineapple, and passion-fruit. If you want to keep it simple, you don't need to serve this in a traditional, curved Hurricane glass, but it does help to have a glass with some volume to it.

Take your tumbler, top it up with ice, and add 50ml (2 measures) dark rum and the same of white rum. Next, add your tropical fruit juice. It helps to have something super-sweet to mix in, such as a flavoured syrup of some sort. That's about it, really. The best way to look at this cocktail is that it's a punch in a glass, using two types of rum.

The traditional drink was developed in the 1940s in New Orleans by a bartender called Pat O'Brien, who made it with lime and passion-fruit. It was consumed enthusiastically by sailors, giving the spirit even more of a link with rum.

This cocktail is very malleable and one bar in particular has made this drink its own. NOLA (which, in local parlance, stands for New Orleans/Louisiana), a London-based bar, pays homage to the first part of its name by having a specific section on its menu dedicated to the New Orleans-invented cocktail, offering five different versions of the Hurricane, not all involving rum. Well worth a visit for a flight of Hurricanes alone.

Meet the Maverick

» JEAN FRANCOIS KOENIG
MEDINE DISTILLERY, MAURITIUS
··
Jean Francois Koenig, master distiller at the Medine
Distillery in Mauritius, creates rums aged in a variety of
casks. His latest release, Penny Blue (*see* p.123), sees a
collaboration of noses and knowledge with Doug McIvor
from the world's oldest wine and spirits merchant, Berry
Bros. & Rudd, based in Mayfair, London.

What is it that makes your rum different from other styles of rum?
"Firstly, I would start with the rum itself. We have been making rums in Mauritius for years, but mainly white rums and light rums. This was our style, consumed as mixers and part of the heritage of Mauritius. In the 1980s, we started to age some rums due to a change in the law. We had to change the distillation, as a light rum wouldn't mature well, so we changed to a heavier style of rum, but distilling it slower and at a lower temperature."

How has the process of maturation been undertaken?
"When we decided to mature rum, we had no traditions, so we tried different things, like ex-Cognac barrels, ex-bourbon barrels, and ex-whisky barrels, really to explore, and we ended up with some very good products, with red fruits and dried fruits. We also found specific differences between the barrels."

Tell us a little about the distillery itself.
"The distillery is producing other products as well as the Penny Blue, but this is the real hand-crafted product we produce in very small quantities. We are on the dry west coast of Mauritius so we end up with cane that has a very high sugar content. The lack of rain gives a greater concentration of sugar and this gives us a good, rich product to work with. We have a specific fermentation process where we slowly add the molasses over time."

What was your main ethos when creating Penny Blue?
"Some people have described this as a whisky-drinker's rum, as it has a drier finish, which gives it a grown-up balance. It is a range of different ages, with the youngest component being four years old and the oldest being 10 years old. It was about getting it balanced from the cask we had available. There were some 'star casks', which were already mature at a young age."

What is the environment like for maturation?
"We have a very hot average temperature and our 'angels' share' is around six per cent a year, so twice that of Scotland and its whisky. Some of our casks are great into old age, but most are good in a short period of time: say, three or five or eight years old."

Describe Penny Blue in three words.
"Innovation, pleasure and conviviality."

» 10 RUMS TO TRY

There are no real rules as to what makes a good rum, save for the usual ones that apply to all spirits. If you are using it for mixing and cocktail work, you might want a white rum or, as is commonly used, a spiced rum to play with. However, if you are looking to have a glass of well-matured rum, then you want to make sure it's balanced, not too sweet nor too bitter, with good body and a decent ABV. You will find that a good rum will accompany anything from a cigar to a good dessert and can make an excellent apéritif.

» LA HECHICERA FINE AGED RUM
40% | Colombia

The Riascos family blends rums from across the Caribbean at its bodega. This extra-aged rum, which is soft, not too sweet, and carries a good level of age, is crafted from rums of 12–21 years of age in a solera system, whereby all the liquid is vatted together so there will always be some very old product in each bottle. The stunning bottle with its blue waxed top is a classy carriage for this rich lady of a rum, named after the Spanish word for "enchantress".

» MAISON LEBLON RESERVA ESPECIAL CACHAÇA
40% | Brazil

Co-founder and master distiller at Leblon, Gilles Merlet employs craft methods such as hand-harvesting sugar cane and using its juice in less than three hours from pressing. Distillation takes place through copper pot stills in small batches, earning Leblon certification as an *artesanal Cachaça de Alambique*. This expression is aged for up to two years in French oak, giving it rich flavours of toasted oak.

» EL DORADO SPECIAL RESERVE 15-YEAR-OLD RUM
40% | *Guyana*

Guyana's only rum-producing distillery is famous for its three wooden stills, all based at the Diamond plantation. El Dorado is made using locally sourced molasses from demerara sugar, which, coupled with Guyana's humid climate, gives a fast-maturing rum with a richness that is beyond its years. This expression is a minimum of 15 years old, but El Dorado is also available in other age statements.

» SANTA TERESA 1796 RON ANTIGUO DE SOLERA RUM
40% | *Venezuela*

Having acquired a copper still in Europe in 1885, Santa Teresa grew its output and has since established itself as one of the foremost producers of rum in Venezuela. Currently it matures in American white oak and French Limousin oak casks. This expression is a solera (*see* left) vatting of rums aged around 15 years. Winning various awards, this rum is all honey and vanilla with hints of spice on the back palate.

» THE KRAKEN BLACK SPICED RUM
47% | *Trinidad and Tobago*

Leading the trend towards exciting, spiced rums, Kraken has developed a strong following in the bartender community. Taking their inspiration from the sea (where else with rum?!), it is named after a mythical sea monster that resembles a giant squid. The rum is distilled in Trinidad and Tobago at the Angostura Distillery, aged for between one and two years, and flavoured with cinnamon, ginger, and cloves.

» PENNY BLUE XO SINGLE ESTATE MAURITIAN RUM
44.1% | *Mauritius*

Penny Blue, which takes its name from a rare and much sought-after Mauritian stamp released in 1847, brings together Jean Francois Koenig, the Master Distiller at Medine Distillery, and Doug McIvor, the spirits buyer at Berry Bros. & Rudd. Created in small batch sizes, this first release is limited to 3,444 bottles, and gives flavours of orange, vanilla, and tropical fruit in rich syrup.

» NOVO FOGO SILVER CACHAÇA ORGÂNICA
40% | *Brazil*

An environmentally friendly and family-run distillery, Novo Fogo is reinventing cachaça for a younger and more vibrant export market, with a specific focus on the USA. Their clear spirit is a smooth example of what can often be quite a harsh product when it hasn't been rested in oak. This edition is matured instead for a year in large stainless-steel tanks, which gives an extra smoothness to the finished spirit.

» RUM SIXTY SIX FAMILY RESERVE
40% | *Barbados*

Produced at the legendary Foursquare Distillery, Rum Sixty Six is distilled from molasses in small batches of around 110 barrels at a time for a minimum of 12 years. Produced from spirit made in both a column still and a more artisanal copper pot still, the rum – which takes its name from the year in which Barbados gained independence from the United Kingdom – is rich and fruity, aided in flavour by fast maturation in American white oak casks.

» BRUGAL 1888 RON GRAN RESERVA FAMILIAR RUM
40% | *Dominican Republic*

Brugal & Co in Puerto Plata produces a variety of rums, but their pioneering expression is Brugal 1888, which is named after the year the distillery launched their first aged rum. The spirit is part-matured in sherry casks, giving a rich and fruity flavour. The bottling is also one of the most "premium" there is, with a heavy metal-topped cork stopper that could be used as a method of self-defence if need be!

» NEISSON RHUM AGRICOLE BLANC
55% | *Martinique*

Founded back in 1931, family-owned Distillerie Neisson is one of the most highly regarded rhum agricole producers in Martinique, still growing its own sugar cane on 34 hectares of land. Their spirit is stored for at least three months in steel vats, allowing it to mellow. The rhum, which is not bottled as *blanc* or white rhum, is matured in oak casks and released at various ages. The *blanc* offering is sweet and smooth, giving hints of icing sugar and vanilla.

WHISKY

Lord of the Grains

SPIRIT NAME	ETYMOLOGY/ COUNTRY OF ORIGIN	COLOUR	MAIN COUNTRIES OF PRODUCTION	BIGGEST-SELLING GLOBAL BRANDS	KEY INGREDIENTS
Whisky – spelled with an "e" in Ireland and widely across America. Believed to have been derived from the Gaelic words *uisge beatha*, meaning "water of life".	Widely debated among historians. It is likely that production was started in Ireland by monks in the twelfth century, travelling over the Irish Sea to Scotland.	Light gold ranging to vibrant chestnut. The colour is determined by the type and length of cask maturation.	USA, Canada, Scotland, Ireland, Japan, Australia, central Europe, and India.	Johnnie Walker, Jack Daniel's, Canadian Club, Glenfiddich, The Glenlivet, Chivas Regal, Jim Beam, and Maker's Mark.	Malted barley in Scotch whisky (maize, wheat, and rye in American whiskey) is fermented and distilled several times, then matured in oak casks.

WHISKY

Lord of the Grains

You might like, or even love, whisky, but what *is* whisky? Aside from spirits as a category in general, which is huge and diverse, whisky as a sub-category goes toe-to-toe in terms of sheer diversity and appeal. So where do we start when it comes to whisky? Well, before we go into production methods, maturation, and blending, we need to sort out one thing: the spelling...

TO "E" OR NOT TO "E"

Whiskey or whisky: do you add or subtract the "e"? This depends, in the main, on where you are in the world. In general, Scottish-made whisky will not use an "e", nor will single malts made in other parts of the world, such as Sweden, Japan, and India. Scotch whisky carries a premium air about it, and for other countries to align themselves with both the production values of the Scotch industry and the spelling of the product gives them reason to compete for the same consumers. When it comes to leaving the "e" in, this tends to be the domain of the Irish and the American producers, with some notable exceptions such as Maker's Mark (a whisky, not a whiskey) or Balcones Texas Single Malt Whisky.

The key is, don't get too hung up on this issue. It's only spelling and the most important thing is not whether you have an "e" in your whisky but some whisk(e)y in your glass. Much like the word "flavour", what matters is not whether it contains the letter "u" but whether the product actually contains any flavour at all. For ease of use, and if for nothing else than to save on ink, we will use the spelling "whisky" for this chapter, unless we are talking about Irish or American products.

On the whole, whisky is a spirit made from any grain-based product, distilled and matured in oak barrels. As with all spirits, the base product will vary and tends to be linked to the location of the whisky and what traditionally would have been farmed in the region where the distillery is located.

SCOTLAND

Whisky's Motherland

Let's start in what is often considered to be the home of whisky, Scotland, where two different types of spirit – malt and grain whisky – are produced from two different base products. Both malt and grain whiskies must be matured in oak casks for at least three years to be legally classed as whisky. This is in order to give the spirit time to mature, taking on flavour and colour. In Scotland, conditions are good for long maturation; the consistently low temperatures mean that the naturally occurring loss of spirit from the casks, known as the "angels' share", is small compared to other whisky-producing countries. Those Scottish angels are clearly the laziest of them all. It is this slow maturation that gives Scotch its premium status within the whisky world.

Malting –
Fast Food for Yeast

The process of malting is very important in whisky. For the yeast to work on creating alcohol, it must digest sugars. Sugars are contained in various cereals, but often in the form of more complex starches, which are harder for the yeast to break down. Malting is the process of turning the starches hidden in, say, barley into shorter, less complex sugars and therefore much more manageable for the yeast to digest. Malting is achieved by creating an environment where barley, the best cereal for malting, is encouraged to grow. These conditions are typically warm and moist. Timing is the key here, as the barley will naturally use up these sugars growing if they are not caught in time. The process is "paused" by heating the barley up to a point where it can no longer grow; it dries out and leaves behind little hand grenades of sugar-filled fun for the yeasts to devour.

MALT WHISKY

The first, which is probably the most recognized around the globe, is single malt, which is made from just three ingredients: water, barley, and yeast at a single distillery and distilled in copper pot stills (*see* p.20). Occasionally these whiskies will be made from barley that has first been smoked with peat. This imparts a smoky flavour to the drink, something that drinkers either love or, erm, don't! The islands of Islay, Skye, and Orkney are the most well-known producers of peated whiskies, with brands like Laphroaig, Ardbeg, Talisker, and Highland Park producing notably smoky spirits, in Laphroaig's case filling your glass with distinct medicinal notes. When it comes to the unpeated style of single malt Scotch, the powerhouse brands of The Glenlivet and Glenfiddich are the biggest-selling single malt whiskies in the world, both exuding a lighter, fresh-fruit note alongside a more palate-pleasing malty sweetness. Scotland has a plethora of single malt whisky distilleries offering a huge variety of flavours. But for the large majority of them, bottling the whisky as a single malt is not their commercial driving force. This is because a large proportion of single malt distilleries exist to provide a key component of blended whisky.

BLENDED AND GRAIN WHISKY

As the name suggests, blended whisky is made up of a mixture of whisky from different single malt distilleries as well as Scotland's other big whisky product, grain whisky. Grain whisky is made at larger production facilities in huge column stills (*see* p.21) using any grain product as its base, and gives a sweeter, lighter flavour than malt whisky. Not as commonly available as single malt, single grain whisky is growing in popularity partly due to the increasing scarcity and rising price of single malt, and partly through the discovery of its easy-drinking nature.

Global sales of single malt Scotch whisky are dwarfed by those of blends (currently around 92 per cent of the worldwide Scotch market), which in turn keep most of Scotland's single malt distilleries open. The likes of Johnnie Walker, Chivas Regal, and Cutty Sark, all huge global brands, have helped shape the growth of whisky worldwide, and allow distillers to bring their single malts to a wider connoisseur market as a result. So when you hear someone criticizing blended whisky, have a word and tell them to drink up.

← *The malting of barley requires heat, which is often provided by the burning of peat, leaving a smoky medicinal flavour.*

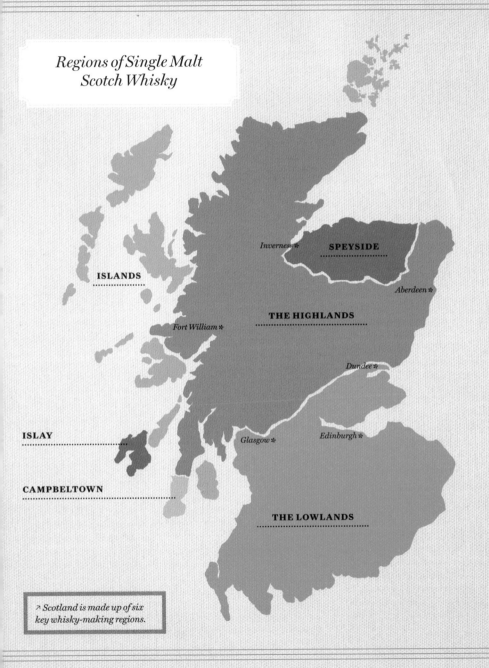

Regions of Single Malt Scotch Whisky

ISLANDS

SPEYSIDE

Inverness ⁕

Aberdeen ⁕

THE HIGHLANDS

Fort William ⁕

Dundee ⁕

ISLAY

Glasgow ⁕   Edinburgh ⁕

CAMPBELTOWN

THE LOWLANDS

↗ Scotland is made up of six
key whisky-making regions.

USA

Whiskey's Adopted Homeland

Although bourbon is considered by many as the native spirit of America, its rich, fragrant history can actually be traced back over 200 years to European settlers and the distillation skills conceived and practised across Scotland, Ireland, and, perhaps more surprisingly, Wales. Yet it undoubtedly carries with it as rich a heritage as Scotch and Irish whiskies – and has witnessed similar highs and lows in its appreciation and consumption. Among the first to establish the production of whiskey in Bourbon County (the name of which is derived from the French royal house, which aided the Americans to defeat the British in the War of Independence) was Evan Williams, who emigrated to America from his homeland of Wales. It is also documented that another very famous name in the world of American whiskey, Mr Jack Daniel, had himself descended from the loins of a Welsh grandfather and a Scottish grandmother.

As Bourbon County grew in stature, so did the legends. The rather thrifty Reverend Elijah Craig purportedly stored his bourbon in used barrels, which

he would char to remove any traces of the previous contents. Over time, as the whiskey was transported across America, it was discovered that this charring process created a wonderfully smooth and mellow spirit, also imparting a rich, dark colour. This tradition came full circle, with American legislation of 1936 dictating that only brand-new charred barrels could be used in the production of bourbon. When they are

↑ *A tall order: Classic column stills can vary dramatically in height between distilleries.*

emptied, the used casks are more often than not shipped to Scotland, where they give single malt Scotch whisky similar fruity, vanilla notes. (For more on using casks, *see* pp.140–1.)

DISTILLING HERITAGE

Bourbon is usually distilled twice, using column stills (*see* p.21) and in a few cases, such as the Woodford Reserve Distillery in Kentucky, pot stills similar to those in Scotland (*see* p.20). One of the most significant differences (and this is where the ears of most American bourbon distillers prick up) is in the yeast strains used to create a fermented mash.

A number of bourbon distillers have painstakingly maintained different yeast strains, some dating way back. Four Roses master distiller Jim Rutledge has traced the distinct flavour connotations each yeast brings to the resulting spirit. This fanaticism links today's bourbon producers with the distant past and their ancestors, and completely affirms that the rich tapestry of American distilling is truly alive with not only fantastic spirit, but characters too.

— Bourbon's Mash-up —

So how is bourbon made? Well, a little differently to how whisky is made in Scotland, that's for sure. For starters, the base spirit is created from not just one ingredient but usually from a trio of grains: maize (corn), rye, and malted barley. This combination is known as the mash bill and, a little like a DNA strand, is different for each bourbon. Each grain, when perfectly balanced, will give a well-rounded, versatile spirit, the individual elements of which can be traced back to the specific flavours each grain is famed for.

Maize

This is the major constituent grain in the mash bill of a bourbon, which, by law, must contain over 51 per cent maize. As well as helping to yield a higher amount of alcohol, maize gives the resulting spirit a particular sweetness... it's not called sweetcorn for nothing. For decades, corn whiskey was the preserve of the illicit distiller, who would sell his unaged white spirit in screw-top jars for very competitive prices. Today, single corn whiskies are becoming popular with bartenders due to their distinctive sweetness. One distillery in particular, the Balcones Distillery, has produced a number of outstanding aged corn whiskies, giving the category a huge kick as a result.

Rye

This is the flavour powerhouse in the production of bourbon. It provides a peppery, spicy, and dry backbone to the mash bill. If you have ever eaten rye bread, you will have tasted the distinct warming note that is imparted to a bourbon. Use too much and the whiskey will be very one-sided, which historically some American distillers have brilliantly capitalized on, releasing specific rye-heavy whiskies. This is a style of American whiskey-making that is very much in favour at the moment, because the big, bold, and individual flavours work incredibly well in classic American whiskey cocktails and sipped over ice.

Malted barley

This helps to marry all the flavours together, itself contributing a rich maltiness to the final spirit. Today, as the number of American craft distillers gathers apace, more are experimenting with American single malt whiskies (not legally classed as bourbons) using malted barley, which have similar characteristics to Scotch whisky but, due to the conditions they are aged in (usually in much hotter temperatures), are developing unprecedented flavour profiles.

Other grains

A number of distilleries (such as the highly popular Maker's Mark) use wheat to give their bourbon an additional creaminess on the palate. But the list doesn't just stop there by any means. Some of the more experimental distillers have begun distilling with a range of ultra-niche grains, including buckwheat, einkorn, millet, Job's Tears, and quinoa, each giving radical alcohol yields and in some cases completely bonkers flavours.

IRELAND – RESURGENT WHISKEY POWERHOUSE

Ireland used to be home to a substantial concentration of whiskey production but was then badly hit during Prohibition. Today it is seeing a resurgence in production, with small distilleries popping up all over the island.

Irish single malt whiskey is becoming increasingly more popular, lead by Bushmills Distillery, located close to the Giant's Causeway in the far north of Northern Ireland.

Down in the south, the real powerhouse of Irish whiskey is to be found. The Midleton Distillery uses huge copper pot stills to create many different varieties of whiskey from a mixed mash bill (the specific recipe for the types of grain used) of both malted and unmalted barley. It is the sheer size of the pot stills at this distillery that means the "cut" of alcohol taken from the distillation will vary in style and flavour. As a result, and with additional levels of maturation in different wood types, Midleton Distillery can produce a number of brands of "single pot still whiskey" all with distinctly different flavour profiles. On top of this, the site can also produce grain whisky and blends such as the hugely popular Jameson blended Irish whiskey, gins, and vodkas.

One common theme across both Bushmills and the Midleton Distillery is that their whiskey is distilled three times, unlike their Scottish counterparts, which (with one notable exception of Auchentoshan near Glasgow) distil twice only. If you ask a Scotch distiller why this is, he will often quip that "the Irish need to do it three times to get it right; we only need to do it twice!" But in reality, triple distillation leads to a lighter style of spirit that matures well and is seen as easy-drinking and mixable in cocktails.

JAPAN – THE RISING WHISKY SUN

Imagine what it would have been like some time in the last two decades for the hypothetical Scottish-based Japanese whisky salesman. His job, attempting to sell the proverbial "coals to Newcastle", would have seemed an impossible task, made even harder as he was dealing with such a highly controversial product in a domestic market steeped in historical pride. Despite this, the salesman persisted, and in a few years Japanese whisky grew steadily in stature, rising from its niche position of interest into a globally accepted, multi-award-winning spirit. Undoubtedly Japanese whisky is one of the real success stories in the category and one that is simply far too important in the flavour stakes to ignore.

The story of Japanese success
Japanese whisky-making can be traced back to the early 1920s and the enthusiasm of two men: Masataka Taketsuru and Shinjiro Torii. Taketsuru-san spent time studying organic chemistry in Scotland, with the view that the secrets to making Scotch could be unravelled and shipped back to Japan, where he would create that country's very first whisky. By spending time at the Hazelburn Distillery, Taketsuru began to understand the intricate processes of how distillation worked and where some of the integral flavours

Blended whisky is also a huge domestic spirit in Japan, and blends such as Hibiki (even if you never taste this beautiful whisky, please Google the bottle design), Kakubin, and Nikka Whisky from the Barrel are enjoyed as wonderfully long, leisurely drinks poured over crystal-clear ice and equally high-quality spring water in what's known as a Highball, or Mizuwari (with still water). If you or your partner/friend has an aversion to the "strength" of whisky, then these simple drinks could prove to be a total revelation in the flavour department – they really work!

Today, these powerhouses dominate the market, with a further four working distilleries making whisky of varying styles and quality. Of these, the most interesting are the Chichibu Distillery, established in 2008 by Ichiro Akuto (*see* p.142–3), and Eigashima – the White Oak Distillery down to the southwest of the country in the Hyogo Prefecture, which have traced their whisky production back to a similar time to that of Yamazaki. Both these micro-distilleries are beginning to make some headway in the marketplace, despite being dwarfed by their respective peers, and today, given the quality of the retailer, you are likely to find bottles of Japanese whisky on the shelves that, in our opinion, will equal anything produced in Scotland and in some instances (hush hush) are perhaps even that bit better.

found in whisky came from. A case of industrial espionage? Perhaps, but his tenacity paid off, and in 1923, alongside Torii he built the first Japanese whisky distillery, later known as Yamazaki, not far from Kyoto. The climate, although warmer than in Campbeltown where the Hazelburn Distillery was located, shared similarities and thankfully it was ideal for slowly maturing casks of whisky.

A revolution of spirit-making had begun, and over the last 90 years Japanese whisky production has grown to be a phenomenon, with Suntory (owner of the Yamazaki and Hakushu Distilleries) competing heavily with Nikka (which Taketsuru established when he parted ways with Torii in 1934, creating the Yoichi and Miyagikyo Distilleries). Each makes single malt whiskies, with explosive palates, showcasing characteristic fruitiness, incense, hints of spice, and in a few cases peatiness, like those whiskies found on Islay in Scotland.

← The enormous pot stills for which Ireland's Midleton Distillery has become famous.
↑ Masataka Taketsuru, often referred to as the Godfather of Japanese Whisky, honed his skills in Scotland.

The Other Whisky Nations

The growth of whisky is not just limited to the four countries previously mentioned. Take a world map and a box of pins and we estimate that you would use about 27 of them (from Australia to Sweden and Taiwan) to highlight all the places that have an active community of whisky-makers. But although the name whisky (taking into account the optional "e") might be the same, the production process, raw materials, wood types, and length of time to mature a finished spirit are all very different. For instance, at the Waldviertler Roggenhof craft distillery in Austria, Johann Haider has pioneered the use of fresh Manhartsberger oak casks, which give the resulting rye and malt whiskies he makes an unusual sweet, sappy fragrance. Some traditionalists will never get to grips with whiskies of this type, as they stray a step too far from the classic profile of what whisky is perceived to taste like. But to others they offer a unique opening into a category that might seem stuffy, outdated, and unapproachable.

→ *Whisky is huge in India but be careful: not all of it is made from grain.*

INDIA – THE LATEST WHISKY FRONTIER
·····································

At the far end of the spectrum lies India, remarkably the biggest whisky-consuming nation in the world. But the majority of what is consumed there could never be classed as whisky as we know and love it. With the exception of a few brands such as the sensational Amrut and Paul John single malt whiskies, most Indian whisky is actually more akin in flavour profile to a sweet rum, mostly down to the fact that its base ingredient isn't a malted cereal at all but in fact molasses. Scary fact time: if one were to take the combined volume sales figures from the four biggest-selling Indian-made whisky brands, they would dwarf the sales of the entire Scotch whisky business internationally. However, because of the rules and regulations that govern whisky-making across Europe and in the USA, you are unlikely to see any of these monster brands on the shelves of your local off-licence.

One thing is for sure: this complex market has a real taste for whisky of all denominations and, as tastes and palates develop, it's going to be an extremely important part of the worldwide renaissance in this wonderful product we all love.

5

Indipensable Whisky Facts

* Whisky in Scotland is spelled without an "e", whereas the Irish and the Americans, on the whole, will use the vowel, spelling it W-H-I-S-K-E-Y.
* The loss in whisk(e)y maturation is known as the "angels' share" and can vary from two per cent per year in Scotland to 10 per cent in hotter countries such as India and America.
* Johnnie Walker is the biggest-selling Scotch whisky brand in the world.
* France is the largest consumer of Scotch whisky by both volume and value in the world.
* Indian whisky is often not made from a malted barley, corn, or rye base but from molasses sugars and a mix of malted barley or other cereal, making it more like a rum than a whisky.

Meet the Maverick

» CHIP TATE
TATE & CO. DISTILLERY, WACO, TEXAS, USA

Look up "maverick" in the dictionary and you'll find a photo of Chip Tate. The founder of Balcones Distillery, Chip has built a reputation as one of the standout innovators in the world of American spirits craft. His new project, Tate & Co., is set to take innovation in distilling to a new level.

What makes Tate & Co. such an unusual distillery?

"In a certain respect, nothing... but also everything! We'll have two large direct-fired stills – we won't be the only distillery to have these, but they're no longer common – and four spirit stills of around 4,000 litres. The lyne arms are unique; that's all I can say about them at the moment. Lots of things that look cool, and will make it tasty too. We'll also be working on our yeast, which really is unique. In summary: Tate & Co. will look cool, and make great whisky!"

What is your ethos in making new spirits?

"I've learnt a lot over the last ten years, and this will the culmination of these experiences. My aim is always to combine flavours in truly new and interesting ways, but to avoid novelty for the sake of novelty. I'll always try to create new spirits that only 'happen' to be new, but could have been created a hundred years ago."

What has been your biggest discovery since running distilleries?

"Apart from the fact it's really hard? Well, it's a little bit like having kids: you know you're diving into something deep, but you just do it and get on with it and look back at what you've done. You also have to invest in the roots. Everything takes time and money, and once you get that right and build on it, you'll be ok. If you form it well, you'll have a good place. Invent, but hold true to traditional standards."

Give us three words that sum up Tate & Co.

"World-class craft distillery."

WHISKY & WOOD

A Match Made in Heaven

No matter where you are in the world, there is one key consistent when it comes to making great whisky and that is top-quality wood. Whisky is a dark spirit, which means that, more than any other spirit in this book, it relies heavily on drawing both colour and flavour from oak casks. These casks can be used a number of times to mature whisky, with the exception of American bourbon whiskey, where the casks must be new oak (virgin oak) and used only once.

RESIDUAL FLAVOURINGS

Each time a cask is used, it will impart less flavour to the spirit maturing inside. Think of the cask like a tea bag – each time you use it, the tea becomes weaker and weaker. Keep thinking about that tea bag, because the contents are also key. If you have a tea bag of traditional English breakfast tea, that's what your cuppa will taste of. But if you have some exotic, green tea from the Far East, you will end up with an entirely different flavour in your mug. This is pretty obvious stuff, really. Because oak is a porous material containing small vessels and veins, when it's filled with any substance, it soaks it up and retains a portion hidden in the wood.

Apart from bourbon, whisky producers around the world are most likely to use casks that have previously been used, often those used for maturing bourbon or European products such as sherry, port, or wines. Using an ex-sherry cask, for example, will give a whisky a rich flavour of dried fruit. Ex-bourbon casks traditionally impart vanilla and white flower tones to the spirit they subsequently hold. This is in contrast to bourbon casked in fresh oak, which gives intense flavours of fresh vanilla pods and tannic, dry, wood spices.

WOOD TYPES

Another dimension that can add to the flavour of whisky is the type of wood used. In Scotland, only oak casks may be used, and the source of the oak will typically be from with the USA or Europe. American oak trees grow straighter than their European counterparts, producing a tighter grain. This in turn gives less of the wood flavour to the spirit and holds less of the previous incumbent of the cask, leading to the lighter style of whisky mentioned earlier. European oak, on the other hand, is much more open, giving greater flavour and intensity to the whisky in the cask.

Experiments are often carried out using different styles of oak such as Nordic or Polish, with Japanese mizunara oak providing one of the best options for maturation outside of the traditional European and American varieties, not just for Japanese distilleries but also for Scottish distilleries. Mizunara grows short and curved, making it a particularly difficult oak to turn into casks, ensuring that the whisky from these rare casks is highly prized.

SIZE MATTERS

The final layer when it comes to wood management, as distilleries call it, is the size of the casks that are used. Put simply, spirit in a small cask will mature much faster than that in a large one, as the surface area to spirit ratio is higher. Let's return to our tea-bag analogy: if you have a large teapot, you need more tea bags to flavour the water.

→ *The most elemental job in whisky: a cooper hard at work toasting a barrel.*

Legally, in Scotland, no cask over 700 litres (154 gallons) in capacity can be used to mature spirit. As whisky must be matured for a minimum of three years and a day to be called Scotch whisky, small casks would mean very fast maturation and the likely ruination of a potential whisky before it can be christened with its true name.

However, there are now some companies, both from the US and Scotland, which are selling small casks of 1–25 litres (1¾ pints–5½ gallons), complete with new-make spirit, for "home maturation". Watch out, however, as these whiskies mature very fast and can often end up tasting pretty awful, even if it is a fun way to see how your spirit matures.

Know Your Wood: Different Sized Casks

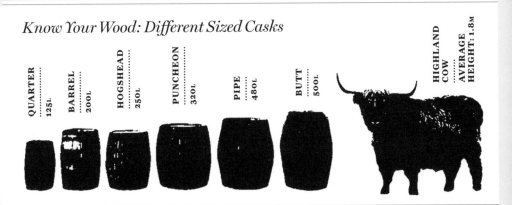

QUARTER 125L — BARREL 200L — HOGSHEAD 250L — PUNCHEON 320L — PIPE 480L — BUTT 500L — HIGHLAND COW AVERAGE HEIGHT: 1.8M

Meet the Maverick

» ICHIRO AKUTO
CHICHIBU, JAPAN
....

Ichiro Akuto, the 21st generation of a long line of Japanese distillers dating back to the seventeenth century, has been a major player in the world of artisanal Japanese whisky for over a decade, well known not only for saving the remaining stocks from the legendary (sadly now defunct) Hanyu Distillery, but for being the man behind Japan's newest whisky distillery Chichibu.

**What makes Chichibu
a unique distillery?**
"Three things: firstly, the
unique circumstances of
being able to build my own
distillery from scratch to my
own specification; secondly, the
passion of the people who work
with me; and thirdly, the fact
that we have gone back to basics
with the way we make whisky
– everything from milling to
distilling is done on one floor."

**What is your ethos in making
new spirits?**
"I'm very conscious of the fact
that Japanese whisky has become
much more high profile, and
as a result, what I'm trying
to do is now very much on
the global stage, so I feel a lot
more conspicuous than if I was
distilling perhaps 20 years ago.
I'm going out of my way to source
the best ingredients and do
things the right way so that I can
continue the success of the other
successful brands out there."

**What has been your biggest
discovery since you began
running a distillery?**
"Well, the core part of making
whisky, such as the actual
fermentation and distillation, is
fairly fixed, but where I've been
able to experiment is outside
of that: from trying out floor
maltings, working with farmers
to grow local barley, or sourcing
my own casks and washbacks
made using Japanese oak."

**Give us three words that
sum up Chichibu.**
"Twenty-first generation
innovation."

*

———

Delectable, Dead-easy Whisky Cocktails

Whisky cocktails are the source of much debate with seasoned aficionados of the spirit. For instance, how sacreligious is it to mix an aged, well-matured single malt whisky into a drink with sweet vermouth, bitters, and lots of ice? Or is breaking an unwritten rule of adding an additional flavour to a classic cocktail recipe acceptable in the name of progress? Frankly, none of these rules apply here, and with the following cocktails, we couldn't care less if they offend the odd sensitive palate out there. They taste superb to us and are dead easy to replicate at home.

Classic Bourbon Mint Julep

Among the greatest bourbon-based cocktails is the Mint Julep, which originated in the Southern state of Virginia, probably as a direct result of the huge bourbon production in the area. The cocktail's simplicity is the key to its longevity, with four very simple ingredients.

INGREDIENTS
....

2 teaspoons granulated sugar
or simple sugar syrup

*

4 sprigs of fresh mint,
plus an extra sprig to garnish

*

2 teaspoons water (omit if using sugar syrup)

*

40ml (1½ measures) quality bourbon
Wild Turkey 101 works well here

METHOD
....

Add the sugar, mint, water, and some crushed ice to a Collins-style glass and muddle together. Then add the bourbon and more crushed ice, stir, and top with the extra sprig of mint. Serve with a straw, a good-looking squeeze with a smile to die for, and a dead cert in the Kentucky Derby. To really give this a positively fruit-laden slap, use a couple of teaspoons of black cherry jam instead of the sugar.

✳
———

Peated Blood & Sand – AKA Hart Peat

This drink takes its name from the 1922 Rudolf Valentino film of the same name, usually calling for blended Scotch whisky as the protagonist. We were once asked to develop some drinks to accompany a rather special Indian meal, and for the venison course we decided to work on a twist on this inspired and refreshing matinee idol of a drink. Using a Lagavulin The Distillers Edition single malt Scotch whisky (famed for its symphonious mix of peat smoke and sweet, oily Pedro Ximenez sherry-influenced flavour, we named the resulting cocktail Hart Peat in homage to the succulent, spicy meat dish the chef had prepared. Oh dear? More roe deer, we hope...

INGREDIENTS

25ml (1 measure) Lagavulin
The Distillers Edition
✳
25ml (1 measure) freshly squeezed blood
orange juice
✳
12.5ml (½ measure) cherry brandy
✳
20ml (¾ measure) Antica Formula
Carpano Vermouth
✳
mint leaf, to garnish

METHOD

Add the ingredients to an ice-filled shaker and shake vigorously until you start to see stars or a hunting horn sound in the background. Strain into a chilled silver goblet (if you have one) and garnish with a single mint leaf.

✳
—

King of Roses

Unashamedly and unapologetically stolen from a long-lost bar, one of London's greats, called Casita. Now a new venue, Home, it is presided over by one of Casita's former bartenders, Oskar (pictured). This delicious combination was created by Casita's owner, Will Foster. Think of this as a tribute to his venue, which gave so much to so many. Yet in such a small space.

INGREDIENTS

50ml (2 measures) Four Roses bourbon
25ml (1 measure) The King's Ginger liqueur
50ml (2 measures) freshly squeezed orange juice
25ml (1 measure) freshly squeezed lemon juice

METHOD

Add all the above to a shaker with ice
(for additional sweetness, add a dash of
gingerbread syrup), shake, and double-strain
into a small Champagne coupe glass.

10

WHISKIES TO TRY

Choosing ten recommended whiskies from the bulging bag of great expressions around the globe is a near-impossible task. So we argued, rejigged and finally agreed that the following are all superb examples of great whisky making, regardless of where they are from: for example, Scotland, Ireland, America, Japan, and also lesser-known whisky locations too.

» **METHOD AND MADNESS SINGLE POT STILL IRISH WHISKEY**
46% | Cork, Ireland

Irish whiskey is in the midst of a renaissance, spearheaded by Jameson and backed up by a host of craft distilleries emerging across Ireland. This, however, is craft innovation at its finest from the highly experienced team at the Midleton Distillery in Cork: a pot still whiskey finished in French chestnut casks. Smooth and easy to drink, yet with a complex palate of honey, nuts and figs.

» **HIBIKI JAPANESE HARMONY BLENDED WHISKY**
43% | Japan

Unless you're a whisky lover who has spent the past five years curled up asleep in a barrel, you'll have read that Japanese whisky is a huge international success story. However it hasn't occurred overnight, and Suntory, the company behind this incredible blended whisky, has had nearly 100 years of practice. Harmony is rich, very fruity and laden with sweet malty notes: perfect for pouring over ice or making up a highball with soda and a slice of lemon.

» ABERLOUR A'BUNADH BATCH 57 SINGLE MALT SCOTCH WHISKY
60.7% | Speyside, Scotland

Aberlour Distillery is located in Speyside, the heartland of Scotch, and is famous for light and approachable whiskies. However, it produces one drink that is so intense, so full of flavour and so rich in texture that it has a unique following of fans across the world. Produced in small batches, bottled at natural strength and matured only in ex-Oloroso sherry casks, expect a powerful whisky with a soft, velvety flavour.

» FOUR ROSES SINGLE BARREL BOURBON WHISKEY
50% | Kentucky, USA

The bourbon by which we measure all others. Four Roses Distillery uses five different yeast strains, giving ten different bourbon recipes. This means that their single barrels can taste quite different to each other, but all with a unique lineage of quality. Each bottling tells you the warehouse where the barrel has been stored, and its unique number. Think cherry jam, strawberries and vanilla. Staggering stuff.

» KAVALAN SOLIST SHERRY CASK, CASK STRENGTH
58.6% | Taiwan

Since it was founded in 2006, the King Car Distillery in Taiwan, known as Kavalan, has astonished single malt connoisseurs around the world with its incredibly complex whiskies, matured in a wide variety of cask types, including this wonderful, heavily sherried beast. Think bold notes of dried figs, rich brown sugar and a dry, nutty finish and you're only some way to describing this masterpiece.

» PAUL JOHN BOLD INDIAN SINGLE MALT WHISKY
46% | Goa, India

Single malt truly is a global product these days, made everywhere from Aberdeen to Australia. Nestled between these two extremes is the Paul John Distillery in Goa, India. Making whisky using six-row barley from the foothills of the Himalayan mountains, this edition is smoked using peat from Islay, the island famous for making smoky Scotch. The result is an easy to drink, lightly peated single malt.

» COMPASS BOX THE SPICE TREE MALT SCOTCH WHISKY
46% | London/Scotland

John Glaser is more than just a mild-mannered indie master blender; he's an alchemist. Compass Box, established over a decade ago, selects some of the most innovative flavours in mature Scotch whisky, balancing wood types and distillery character to perfection to create highly unusual blends. Spice Tree (think cinnamon spice, robust red fruit, rich demerara sugar) is just one example of why blends are officially cool.

» STARWARD AUSTRALIAN SINGLE MALT WHISKY
43% | Melbourne, Australia

The march of great single malt whisky made in Australia has focused on the island of Tasmania, where distilling has really taken hold. Not to be outdone on the mainland, Starward Distillery started up in Melbourne to produce a malt whisky that is cleverly matured in various sizes of Australian wine casks, and the result is stunning. Notes of jam, prunes and stardust. No, really.

» BAIN'S CAPE MOUNTAIN WHISKY
43% | South Africa

Named after road engineer Andrew Geddes Bain, who pioneered the awe-inspiring Bainskloof Pass, this grain whisky, distilled by the James Sedgwick Distillery in Wellington, has all the zest and vanilla-custard-filled glory you would expect. Column distilled, matured in first-fill American oak, and then bottled at five years old, it is young, vibrant and fresh. Think marzipan, sugar-coated almonds, and ripe nectarines. Stunningly sunny!

» STAUNING PEATED SINGLE MALT WHISKY
53.1% | Stauning, Denmark

Over in Denmark, the Stauning distillery has explored the complex flavours of smoky whisky, taking both barley and peat from Denmark, "smoking" it at their distillery and maturing it in ex-Bourbon American oak barrels – to stunning effect. The result is akin to a peated Scotch from bygone era: sandalwood, vanilla, oak, sweet smoke and moss back up this awesome barley spirit.

FRENCH
BRANDY

Goddess of the Spirit World

SPIRIT NAME	ETYMOLOGY/ COUNTRY OF ORIGIN	COLOUR	MAIN COUNTRIES OF PRODUCTION	BIGGEST-SELLING GLOBAL BRANDS	KEY INGREDIENTS
Brandy. The name is believed to come from the Dutch word for the spirit, *brandewijn*, meaning "burned wine", dating back to the twelfth century, but its origins are likely to go back as far as the very birth of distillation.	Difficult to say, as the history of distilling fruit and grapes has such an undefined past, but brandy production has been widely adopted across Central Europe.	Wide ranging. Crystal clear for some fruit brandies and other eaux-de-vie to dark copper for oak-aged XO Cognac and Armagnac.	France. While brandies and eaux-de-vies are produced across the whole country, the key brandies are Cognac, Armagnac (from the Gascony region), and Calvados (from Lower Normandy).	Hennessy, Courvoisier, Rémy Martin, Martell, Janneau, and Père Magloire.	With the exception of fruit brandies, such as Calvados, the production of French brandies involves distilling grape wine. Some brandies are made from pomace, the leftover skins and pips from wine production.

FRENCH BRANDY

Goddess of the Spirit World

In the universe of spirits, brandy doesn't represent just an entire planet but more of a complete solar system. In fact, given just how popular it is, by rights this book could easily be twice as long, accommodating every single permutation of this most worldly spirit. For the sake of clarity, brevity, and our livers, we have decided to concentrate on some of the most well-known types of French brandy in this section, highlighting the exquisite differences there are between them and just why they have been enjoyed for centuries. Some other spirits, such as grappa and pisco (both of which are technically brandies), have such a rich heritage that we simply couldn't condemn them to a mere footnote and have therefore given them their very own chapter (*see* World Brandies, pp.180–97).

In layman's terms, brandy represents any spirit that is made from either a grape base or, in numerous cases, a particular fruit, each base ingredient bringing its individual personality and flavour to the proceedings. From a variety of locations across the globe, including France, South Africa, South America, and many other European countries, brandy takes on many guises: from heavy, oak-influenced and well-matured examples to fresh, crystal clear, unaged varieties designed to highlight the distinct heritage and culture of the producers, alongside the vibrancy of the ingredients from which they are distilled.

As a result, brandy cannot be pigeonholed with a distinct flavour profile, a classic serve, or a set of rules that surround its production, and the culmination of centuries of experience alongside brandy's triumphant voyages around the globe has meant that the spirit possesses an extraordinary resilience wherever it is enjoyed.

THE BEGINNINGS OF BRANDY

While it's almost impossible to pinpoint the exact birthplace of brandy, we can assume that where there was wine and distillation, there would almost certainly be a spirit resembling an early, crude form of brandy. The ancient Greeks were purveyors of many a fine wine (often enjoying a slightly watered-down glass at breakfast time) and it is likely that wine was distilled as early as 1000 BC, predominantly for medicinal usage. Likewise, later on in the seventh and eighth centuries, wine and other fruit extracts were distilled by Arab alchemists to produce medical preparations, but there is no distinct evidence that the spirit was actually designed for consumption. Yet the spread of knowledge in the processes of distillation (largely throughout European monasteries – see pp.16–18) would lead to a wider understanding and appreciation of grape- and fruit-based spirits, especially in the midwest of France, which had the perfect soil and climate for growing exceptional varieties of grapes. It is recorded that wine was being distilled in French monasteries as early as 1250 (where the name "eau-de-vie" was first used), predating much of the distillation of beers across the Channel in Britain and Ireland to make the first whisk(e)y.

As wine merchants from England and Holland began to import and export wines in the sixteenth century, they hit on the idea of reducing the volume of liquid in each barrel to evade the high taxes levied and limit the amount of cargo carried across the sea. And by boiling the wines, they effectively reduced the water content, which would be topped up when the wine reached its final destination. The name "brandy" is believed to have derived from this fairly insalubrious practice, coined by the Dutch as *brandewijn*, or "burned wine".

COGNAC

France's Most Regal Brandy

Back in France, a revolution of another kind was brewing – or should we say, distilling? – and for the residents of Cognac (the *Cognaçais*), the perfect conditions for growing neat terraces of grape vines would prove to be a life-changing moment. The town of Cognac was built on the banks of the river Charente, which had become an essential waterway for the trade of wine, allowing easy access to the Atlantic, and with it, trade routes across Europe.

Along with the popularity of French wine came Cognac, which was most likely first distilled around 1450, but it was during the seventeenth century that distillers became more skilful at refining the process of producing spirit from the wines grown around the region. They began to practise the art of double distillation, first filling their alembic stills – similar in style to the copper pot stills used in Scotland (*see* p.20) but much more squat in size – with wine, then redistilling the first run of the spirit to obtain a purer spirit with a higher ABV.

In fact, the story goes that one evening, a famous brandy producer dreamed that the devil tried to boil him twice in order to extract his soul. On waking (no doubt needing a stiff measure of brandy to calm his nerves), he realized that he should try to distil his brandy twice, thus extracting its soul. Clearly, the devil's in *le détail*!

As the Cognac was transported on long journeys by sea, the oak casks used to store it began to mature and, rather like the Scots accidentally discovering the effect of wood on their national spirit, the French began to recognize what a beautifully delicate and balanced spirit they had created.

Today, the Cognac industry is big business, and once-humble, family-owned brands are now global powerhouses producing millions of litres a year. But there are still plenty of single estates across the region – essentially small landowners, farmers, and distillers producing very limited quantities of spirit that rarely see the light of day outside of the Cognac region.

REIGN OF TERROIR

Let's get one thing straight. The French are brilliant at protecting and reinforcing the legacy of their own wines and spirits, and back in 1909, the Cognac region became what's known as a "demarcated" area. So, rather like sparkling wine produced in the Champagne region, only brandy produced in the region can legally be called Cognac. But what makes Cognac such a supremely brilliant spirit is largely down to how the region has been carved up into distinct bands of quality, or *cru* – where the soil and the grape vines are earmarked for greatness and the spirit that is produced from the grapes takes on a range of distinctly different flavour profiles. Over in Mexico, you will find a similar terroir effect with the agave plants used to make Tequila and mezcal (*see* p.78).

← *For hundreds of years, Cognac has enjoyed a greater international success than its other spirited French siblings.*

THE WHO'S WHO *CRU'S CRU* OF

Cognac

❊ The most top-flight, high-quality, and most sought-after grapes come from the Grande and Petite Champagne areas, marked out as the fields and terraces nearest the town of Cognac. The chalky soil (where the word *Champagne* comes from) gives the distillates a robust, complex flavour that ages well in oak casks.

❊ Borderies and Fin Bois are both areas that are slightly further out from the centre of Cognac and produce very different flavours. Borderies brings delicate floral and fruit flavours to the proceedings, and Fin Bois a softer fruitiness. They may lack the X factor of the top flight but are largely excellent grapes producing fine Cognacs.

❊ Grapes from the Bon Bois and Bois Ordinaire, an area that extends up to the west coast of France, produce much lighter-style spirits that don't tend to age well and lack the depth of complexity when compared to the other regions.

The grape varieties themselves have another huge impact on the overall flavour of the finished Cognac, and by law, the large majority of spirit produced in Cognac comes from three distinctly different varieties. As wines, they are fairly acidic and low in alcohol (around 8–9% ABV), so particularly uninspiring on the palate, and as a result it is unlikely that you will see them appear on the menu at your favourite French restaurant. But begin to distil them and that's when they start to find their true potential.

❊ **UGNI BLANC**
The star player that provides a high percentage of volume in the make-up of a Cognac and also gives a robust backbone of flavour besides ageing exceptionally well.

❊ **FOLLE BLANCHE**
The ballet dancer if you like: delicate, temperamental, and difficult to grow, but take it away and you would miss its wonderfully delicate floral notes.

❊ **COLOMBARD**
Another lighter, acidic grape variety, less popular than Folle Blanche or Ugni Blanc but very useful in helping the blend of distillates hang together. Due to the lower yields of wine compared to Ugni Blanc, both Folle Blanche and Colombard have taken more of a back seat for the producers of Cognac.

DISTILLATION AND MATURATION

The wines are fed into copper alembic stills and double distilled, with the alcohol strength rising from 8–9% ABV to 68–72% ABV. The spirit is then transferred to oak casks and begins to interact with the wood, mellowing and developing its distinct flavour profile. The type of oak used is important. Casks made from the fine-grained sessile oaks grown in the Tronçais forests of France give an aromatic, less tannic note, whereas Limousin pedunculate or English oak trees have a wider grain, allowing the spirit to soak deep into the staves and extract a drier, oakier character. Legally, a Cognac must mature in oak for over two years.

Older Cognacs develop characterful fruity, floral, vanilla notes: dried fruit and spiciness, combined with a hint of dryness. When the distiller feels that the wood is about to contribute an undesirable effect to the spirit (such as bitter, dry, brittle flavours), it is removed from its oaky slumber and transferred into glass demi-johns, where it can remain, in a spirit form of stasis, until given the seal of approval.

For the cellar master, picking particular vintages and styles of eaux-de-vie and putting together a unique blend is the driving force behind a great Cognac, and some older, more costly bottlings can contain up to 40–50 different individual Cognacs.

CLASSIFYING COGNAC

When looking at the labelling on a bottle of Cognac, there can be a dizzying array of important terms and abbreviations that classify the age, quality, and style of the Cognac. In 1865, Maurice Hennessy, one of the founding generations of the hugely popular brand, introduced a system of classifying a Cognac's age by a simple star rating. The BNIC (*Bureau National Interprofessionnel du Cognac*) has expanded on these humble beginnings with a series of abbreviated descriptions. Interestingly, despite its clear French origins, English words are used in many of the descriptions, primarily because a large number of Cognac exporters were English, supplying a hugely buoyant – and thirsty – market back in Blighty.

VS Stands for "Very Special". The youngest Cognacs produced fall under this category and have to be matured in oak for a minimum of two years.
VSOP Stands for "Very Superior Old Pale". Must contain eau-de-vie aged for a minimum of four years but where the average age is usually much older.
XO Stands for "Extra Old". The youngest eau-de-vie must be at least six years old, but the Cognac will often contain older spirit upwards of 20 years.
Napoleon Usually represents a range of bottling between the XO and VSOP age ranges.

Other distinctions such as *Vieille Réserve* ("Old Reserve") and *Hors d'Age* ("Beyond Age") are often used to describe Cognacs of exceptional age and quality beyond the XO category.

Meet the Maverick

» **ERIC FORGET**
CELLAR MASTER, HINE COGNAC, JARNAC, FRANCE
....

Hine has been making Cognac for over 250 years in the sleepy town of Jarnac on the banks of the river Charante (*see* p.179). The company was founded by Thomas Hine, an Englishman hailing from Dorset, and unlike any other Cognac house, Hine still has a unique relationship with Bristol in southwest England, where they mature a proportion of their casks – resulting in a truly well-travelled spirit!

For you, what does the art of blending different Cognacs together mean?
"That I can deliver a wider palate of aromas and flavours – a blend that is always richer than a unique batch. The more I use different Cognacs, the more complex the blend."

Hine has a long history associated with maturing casks in Bristol. How did the concept (known as "Early Landed") come about?
"We wanted to continue the historical habit from the nineteenth century, where casks would be shipped over to Bristol before being sold. By continuing to do this, we maintain the tradition and offer something unique and very different in flavour, because the ageing

conditions are totally different in the UK to Jarnac (more humid, certainly colder, but with less fluctuation). The result is a Cognac that is more expressive on the nose but still lively and floral, because there is far less impact from the cask."

For the uninitiated, describe the best way to enjoy a fine vintage Cognac and what to look for on the palate.
"A Cognac vintage must be appreciated and described in the same way as a fine wine, and like a wine, the vintage

will always be at the mercy of the weather conditions, despite the distillation process. The description should use the same words that we use for wine tasting. Always take a smaller sip than with a wine and look for the body, the length of time the flavours last, the sweetness, how silky and velvety the texture is, and the absence of harshness and bitterness. Then try to imagine what the weather was like when the Cognac was made!"

What's the best part about being a master cellar master?
"Tasting and blend-making, which involve all my senses!"

Describe the ethos of Hine in three words.
"Delicate, complex, floral."

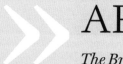

ARMAGNAC

The Brandy That Time Forgot

We would be fairly willing to bet that if we asked you to name France's most popular brandy before reading this chapter, you would correctly answer Cognac. But would you have realized that this most seasoned French campaigner was actually born AFTER another of France's best-kept spirited secrets?

Like that of Cognac, the history of Armagnac has very much been influenced by the terroir of rural southwest France, and as a spirit it is so often overshadowed by its more well-known sibling, simply because Armagnac has yet to gain as significant a foothold outside of France. But when it comes to sitting down with a glass of both of these majestic French brandies side by side, it becomes apparent that any similarities are (grape) skin deep, much in the same way that both Irish and Scotch whiskies have unique aspects to their personalities.

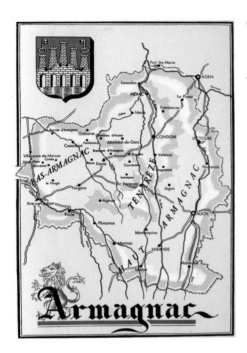

REGIONAL DIFFERENCES

Armagnac (a county of Gascony) lies about 250km (155 miles) south of Cognac and is centred around three important areas, which, like the *crus* of Cognac, help to determine the inherent character and, in many cases, desirability of the spirit. The chilling winds from the Pyrenees force the vines to work hard in the winter months, and the terroir ensures that Armagnac develops a much bolder, more distinct character than that of Cognac. It is here that Armagnac stakes out its roots: producers proudly list the region that their Armagnac is from, as the type of soil in the various regions produces very different results.

Armagnacs from the Bas-Armagnac area are among the most highly prized and elegant spirits, and the area makes up around 57 per cent of all the spirit produced in the region, next to the spirits produced in Tenareze region, which is famed for its chalky soil and very robust, earthy flavours. Finally, a handful of brandies are produced in the Haut-Armagnac region, a large area of land that surrounds the other two in a pincer movement, but one where the wineries are spread few and far between.

> ⌐ *The Armagnac region is split into three distinct production areas, with spirits from the Bas-Armagnac being the most highly sought after.*

Cognac embraces the art of the blend; the alchemy of bringing together flavours from entirely different decades and winemakers, whereas Armagnac takes a much more rustic approach, celebrating the individuality of not only the people who produce it but the landscape that it is rooted within.

Armagnac was established in France at least 150 years before Cognac, and one particular piece of writing from 1310, the *40 Virtues of Armagnac* by Franciscan theologian Vital du Four, seemingly alludes to its magical and medicinal properties.

Armagnac again favours the Ugni Blanc grape, which helps provide a solid backbone to the spirit, alongside the more delicate, temperamental Folle Blanche. But what makes the spirit unique is the Baco grape, which was introduced to the region in the late nineteenth century and today provides much of the complexity found in Armagnac. Although it makes a lousy table wine, when Baco becomes a spirit, it comes out fighting, especially when aged.

SO WHY IS ARMAGNAC ANY DIFFERENT TO COGNAC?

Despite having much in common with Cognac, one of the most striking reasons why Armagnac represents all that is great in the spirits world comes down to the rustic nature of its production. In a world that celebrates consistency, automation, and progress, Armagnac positively worships the antiquated, the outdated, and the artisan way of life.

Armagnac is distilled in a very different way to Cognac and the stills used in its production look like they have been lifted straight out of a Jules Verne novel. Many of them still operate using wood-fired furnaces, which are loaded with unwanted grape vine posts and lit by hand (and occasionally from the butt of the distiller's cigar, it must be said, all you eagle-eyed 'elf and safety experts…)

The stills, based on the traditional column type (*see* p.21), are made up of a number of copper plates through which the wine slowly permeates, with the spirit eventually reaching around 55% ABV, when it is condensed back into a liquid by the "serpentine", or time-honoured worm tub. This single distillation process means that many more of the robust flavours of the wine are retained, rather than being distilled away a second time like the pot-still process practised in Cognac (*see* p.161). During the distillation

ARMAGNAC
CHATEAU HENRI IV

SOCIÉTÉ DES PRODUITS DE L'ARMAGNAC
SIÈGE SOCIAL, CONDOM (Gers)

period, which, by law, operates between November and March, some of the smaller wineries are visited by distillers towing their ancient-looking copper-riveted beasts on the back of a tractor, rather than the wines being carted off to a particular distiller, which makes the process unique and totally idiosyncratic. Have still, will travel.

THE FLAVOURS OF ARMAGNAC

Because of the distinct regionality of production, Armagnac is comparable to single malt whisky produced in Scotland, where the styles are markedly different. For example, the robust, smoky flavours in an Islay whisky are refreshingly different to those found in a classic Speyside whisky.

Coupled with the number of tiny producers (some just filling a handful of casks per year), you will find an array of flavours.

Older vintages from Tenareze and Bas-Armagnac can be big, bold, earthy, and hugely tannic, with a distinct "rancio"-like quality – a highly prized musty/savoury note often found in very complex single malt whiskies matured in sherry casks.

The contrast is that younger Armagnac shares a little more in common with Cognac, offering lighter, more fruity and less complex aromas and flavours that develop in the glass, with vanilla notes, fresh orchard fruit, and hints of woody spice.

Recently, an entirely new category of Armagnac was introduced that showcases the naked spirit, so to speak. Unaged Armagnac eau-de-vie is completely clear, bottled as it runs from the still, and contains an extremely fresh and vibrant profile, with a clean, crisp precision on the palate and a very fruity nose. It makes a great long drink too – perfect for celebrating the tradition of long, lazy summer days spent in the French countryside.

↖ An old Armagnac poster showing a regal man quaffing the spirit on horseback.
→ Some of the oldest bottles of Armagnac in the world at the Dartigalongue Bas-Armagnac Estate, dating back to 1829.

Armagnac de la Réglte
1829
Origine Château Gastou Fils
Réservé en 1858 par Henri Gastou,
grand-père actuelle de Pierre Dartigalong

Meet the Maverick

» MARC DARROZE
DARROZE ARMAGNAC, ROQUEFORT, BAS-ARMAGNAC

Marc Darroze (pictured above left) shares an intriguing kinship with another of our mavericks, Ron Cooper of Del Maguey Mezcal (*see* pp.76–7). Both men have changed the landscape of their respective industries by highlighting the unique aspects of spirit production across a number of single estates and farms.

What are the three most important things you look for when sourcing new casks of Armagnac?

"We actually have two different ways of sourcing great Armagnacs. Some producers are very stable and consistent, and we have long-term relationships with them where we distil some wine on their estates every year. We have created a kind of club where we have a training programme that includes visits to other companies outside the Armagnac area. Our idea is to show producers how important it is to maintain and improve the quality of our Armagnacs. They are all very proud to be a part of our story. But we also have some 'spot' purchases from time to time – often old producers who had distilled and aged in their own facilities a long time ago, or a younger generation who have received a stock of Armagnac from their parents or grandparents."

Do you prefer great age, or character in the Armagnac?

"They are both very important. Because we have such differing soil types, different grapes varieties, our unique distillation methods, and oak cask selection, it allows Armagnac producers to craft brandies with a strong identity and character. We always make choices to highlight these characters. An Armagnac using the Baco grape variety, grown in a sandy soil, then single-distilled at 53% and matured in classic Armagnac casks, will make a unique product. We bottle them exactly as they are to protect the original character of the brandy."

What legacy do you hope to create with the company in the future?

"Ha! A very difficult question. I received from my father the passion for our region and our spirits. I also took on a company built on a special philosophy. We are, how we say in French, artisan. My goal is really to continue this image but also to be modern and forward-thinking, as well as respectful of our history and all the people who are working in Armagnac."

Describe Armagnac Darroze in three words.

"Diversity, respect, pleasure."

CALVADOS

The Intoxicating Essence of the Apple

With the whole of France pretty much resembling a deliciously mouthwatering gastronomic map made up of cheese, pâté, the dangerously moreish Agen prunes, and, of course, fine wines, Cognac, and Armagnac, the area of Normandy has a particular association with the humble apple. Here, a noble cider has been produced since the seventh century, and with it, France's other outstanding style of brandy – Calvados.

The Pays d'Auge region has a particular celebrity about it and it is treated with the same respect as the Grande Champagne region in Cognac country, with in excess of 200 different apple varieties, from sweet and bittersweet to more acidic ones each contributing to the end product, used by distillers year after year to create a consistent blend of flavours. What makes Calvados such a distinct spirit is the inherent link with the cider, which in the Pays d'Auge region must be fermented for at least six weeks, producing a punchy, pungent yet extremely fruity result. The very best Calvados producers will then age their ciders further to intensify the various apple flavours.

Like Cognac, the best Calvados is double-distilled in similar alembic-style copper stills and aged in oak for no less than two years. New-oak casks are gently toasted and in the first three months of maturation the spirit will begin to absorb many of the natural vanillins and tannins from the fresh wood, which can eventually become an undesirable trait if left to develop for too long. Here, the rapidly ageing Calvados is transferred into older casks, where the oak has less of a pronounced effect.

CALVADOS FLAVOUR PROFILES

After two years, the spirit is still vibrant, crisp, and rich in clean fruit flavours, with young Calvados making an exceptional long drink when combined with a fiery ginger beer (*see* p.172 for another refreshing suggestion), but the spirit enters the realms of the sublime when left to sit for a few more years of maturing. After five to six years it becomes more creamy on the palate, with a softening of the zesty, tart apple flavours, and upwards of 15–20 years you are in tarte tatin territory, with delicious spiced notes appearing from the wood alongside buttery cooked-apple notes, fat vanilla pods, and a rich, unctuous thickness on the palate.

Alongside the celebration of *la pomme*, the Normandy region has also given legal recognition to its branch-dwelling neighbour *la poire*, the pear, and a little further southwest lies the Domfrontais area, where Calvados made using a minimum mixture of 30 per cent pear/apple cider is distilled, predominantly once in column stills, giving a cleaner, less flavoursome spirit that reaches its ageing potential more quickly but perhaps lacks the depth of complexity that its neighbours in Pays d'Auge can attain.

Like Armagnac, Calvados has lacked the international exposure of Cognac, but there is a wealth of truly exceptional examples that deserves greater recognition.

MARC – THE FRENCH GRAPPA

While we are really getting our teeth into the tastier aspects of rural France, we might as well touch upon another grape brandy, made in a totally different way to either Cognac or Armagnac, this time using pomace, the skins and pips left over from a grape harvest (*see* above). Marc is rarely seen outside of France and is popular in the Burgundy, Champagne, and Alsace regions, where the leftovers from the harvest of Pinot Noir, Chardonnay, and Gewurztraminer wines are distilled and occasionally aged, with the end result resembling a fresh, grappa-like brandy, and the grape variety heavily influencing the flavour profile.

✻
—

How Best to Enjoy Brandy

With such a wealth of great spirits, French brandies have formed the heart of classic drinks for the better part of two-and-a-half centuries as well as being sipped and savoured alongside cigars and full-fat, unpasteurized cheeses and other delicacies that are probably bad for us.

While there is nothing inherently wrong with the traditional image of brandy (save for the appallingly designed brandy balloon, which we are on a quest to crush decisively forever, before its bulbous curves shock another nose into submission), brandy needs to move on and find favour with a new generation of drinkers.

Using a tulip-shaped nosing glass will infinitely improve the vibrancy of an aged brandy, and allowing it to interact with the air will help to release far more aromas. Cognac and Armagnacs bottled at 40% ABV usually don't need the addition of water to open up, and the more gentle notes are quite easily drowned out if the spirit is diluted.

But the face of French brandy is changing, and with it come a number of expressions that are aimed specifically at the cocktail world. A youthful Calvados, lighter, more floral VSOP Cognac, or unaged blanche Armagnac work superbly in longer drinks. Here's just a small selection to try at home.

Calvados Spritzer

It's barbecue time. You are about to reach for the well-poured gin bottle while the other hand is in the door of the fridge hovering over your tonic water. Stop!

✻

Instead, fill a wine glass full of crushed ice and pour over a double measure of Calvados (a younger style such as Daron Fine or Berneroy Fine will do nicely here and won't break the bank). Add a couple of dashes of Angostura bitters (for more about making your own bitters, *see* pp.214–15) and top the glass up with sparkling water (or for a slightly sweeter version, add a splash of tonic). Garnish with a slice of green apple and locate your Panama hat while taking a lingering sip, before turning your attention to the rapidly charring sausages.

✳
———

The Hine Line

This is a little something we whipped up for a vintage cocktail party, based on a classic Champagne cocktail. The delicate floral notes of the Cognac pair well with the fruity sweetness of the apple juice (if you prefer a drier cocktail, leave out the honey), and the bitters add a welcome hint of spice.

INGREDIENTS

37.5ml (1½ measures) H by Hine VSOP Cognac

✳

37.5ml (1½ measures) quality apple juice

✳

6.25ml (¼ measure) light honey

✳

2 dashes Angostura Bitters

✳

Champagne, to top up

✳

maraschino cherry, to garnish

METHOD

Shake the Cognac, apple juice, honey, and bitters with ice, then strain into a chilled flute, top up with Champagne, and garnish with a maraschino cherry.

✳
—

Blanche Martini

Devilishly simplistic, this is all about celebrating the beautiful freshness found in a blanche-style Armagnac, which is bottled straight from the still at around 50% ABV. Older oak-aged Armagnacs make perfect contemplative sippers (as well as a knockout Old Fashioned), but the new kid on the block in Gascony is most definitely aimed at turning a few heads in the cocktail market.

Start by rinsing out a Martini glass with dry vermouth (Noilly Prat, or for a sweeter take, Lillet Blanc). Add a gentleman's pour (roughly 65ml, or 2½ measures) of blanche Armagnac (*see* p.178) into a mixing glass full of cubed ice, stir for 20–30 seconds, then strain into the glass. Garnish with a thin slice of lemon zest.

» 10

FRENCH BRANDIES TO TRY

With the sheer number of exceptional brandies being produced right across France choosing just "10 to Try" is a very tall order indeed. But for us, the following undoubtedly represent just how important France is and why the French are top of the tree (or grape vine) when it comes to producing exceptional brandy.

» GUILLON-PAINTURAUD VIEILLE RÉSERVE COGNAC
40% | Segonzac

This single-estate producer, based at the heart of the Grande Champagne region, is unusual in that all its Cognacs are made from only one year's production. This contains eaux-de-vie from around 20 years of age. A wonderful aroma of walnuts, soft brown sugar, and slight notes of leather mix with a nutty palate, with chocolate, hazelnuts, and vanilla. An exceptional example of what small producers can deliver.

» CHÂTEAU DE PELLEHAUT BLANCHE ARMAGNAC
44% | Montréal du Gers

A totally new take on the concept of Armagnac, which is better known as a well-aged spirit. Blanche is a refreshing unaged (and therefore clear) Armagnac that has been produced predominantly for mixing. The heady aroma and flavour of fresh plums, apple, stewed prunes, and tarte tatin make this an accessible choice for the Armagnac virgin looking for a superb excursion from the usual Vodka and Tonic.

» H BY HINE VSOP COGNAC
40% | Jarnac

Travel to Jarnac during harvest time and you will still see a producer doing things its way – the way it has operated for the last 250 years (*see* pp.162–3). However, H By Hine represents a departure for Cognac, and this delightfully soft expression (made from grapes grown in the Grande and Petite Champagne regions only) is great sipped on its own or in a cocktail. Vanilla, dried fruit, and subtle oak make this an ideal introduction to the spirit.

» CAMUS VSOP BORDERIES COGNAC
40% | Cognac

The Cognac region is famed for having several different areas, with the Grande Champagne area generally the most sought-after. However, don't forget the other regions, which grow a different style of grape. The Borderies, the smallest cru in the Cognac region, is home to the Camus house, which draws its style from this most craft of areas. Light and easy to drink, this is a winner.

» ARMAGNAC DELORD HORS D'AGE
40% | Lannepax

Surprisingly, this tiny Armagnac house produces around 100,000 bottles a year. What's remarkable is that the bottling process, labelling, and finishing touches (wax sealing and gold embossing) are all done by hand by a team of two or three workers – artisanal production at its best. This 15-year-old has subtle wafts of elderflower, milk chocolate, and dried fruit mixed with maple syrup and candied orange notes on the palate.

» DARROZE LES GRANDS ASSEMBLAGES ARMAGNAC 30 YEARS OLD
43% | Roquefort

Under current custodian Marc Darroze, this pioneering outfit has assembled a huge selection of vintages, each one from grapes produced by specific farmers, alongside bottlings ranging from 10–60 years old (*see* pp.168–9). This is an explosion of citrus fruit, fresh cherries, and marzipan, with a heavy woody influence and liquorice spiciness on the palate.

» ARMAGNAC CASTARÈDE 1939 VINTAGE
40% | Mauleon, Gers

Alongside some sensational younger spirits, notably the 10-year-old VSOP and 20-year-old Hors d'Age, proudly family-owned Castarède prides itself on producing exceptional vintage bottlings. Expensive but truly one of the greatest spirits in the world, this shows an explosion of tropical fruit, dark sugar, vanilla, and earthy spices. A sublime moment if ever there was one.

» DUPONT VIEILLE RÉSERVE CALVADOS
42% | Pays d'Auge

It feels like an injustice to call Calvados France's third best-known brandy, especially when you try this "Old Reserve" from the Dupont family. Aged in oak for five years (with a quarter of the casks being brand-new oak, giving huge tannic structure), a blend of 80 per cent bittersweet and 20 per cent sour acidic apples is fermented for up to six months before being distilled, giving a very distinct note of zestiness, spice, and intense apple.

» ADRIEN CAMUT PRIVILÈGE CALVADOS
40% | Pays d'Auge

Another family-owned Calvados distillery that adheres to the rustic traditions of craft distillation, using around 25 varieties of apples for the cider (which is aged for about 10 months), and firing the tiny stills with wood from the apple trees. This example is aged for 18 years and balances rich, buttery, stewed fruit, vanilla, and sweet honey, with a surprisingly crisp backbone of green apples.

» G. MICLO MARC D'ALSACE DE GEWURZTRAMINER
45% | Alsace

A curve ball in the world of well-known French brandies, we had to include this for sheer intrigue alone. This marc, made from the pomace or leftovers from the harvested Gewurztraminer grapes (*see* box, p.171), offers all the sweet, soft fruit of a quality Alsace white wine (think apricot, a touch of nectarine, and acacia honey), but also delivers a spritely, fresh kick alongside the richness.

WORLD
BRANDIES

Liquid Gold of the Globe

As we mentioned in the previous chapter, brandy has, over the past 500 years, infiltrated every corner of the earth, fusing together individual, international flavours and traditional production methods. Part of its success lies with the brilliant sustainability of the grape vine and the huge interest in New World wine, meaning that grape brandies from Europe, South Africa, and the Americas are becoming more popular than ever. Similarly, fruit brandies can be made from almost anything with a naturally high-sugar (fructose) content, from traditional orchard fruit – generally plums, apples, pears, apricots, or cherries – through to the more exotic stuff: anyone tried brandy made with the kukumakranka fruit in South Africa?

The beauty of brandy or, to give the category a wider moniker, eau-de-vie, is that anything sweet that can be fermented has a good chance of becoming a palatable spirit when in the right hands. Throughout this chapter you will find a few undisputed experts who have most definitely mastered the art of turning fruit (and grapes for that matter) into liquid gold.

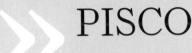

PISCO

The Rising Star of South America

Ask anyone to name the true spirit of the Americas and they will probably say bourbon whiskey from the USA or Tequila from Mexico. But pisco, the quiet son of South America, is slowly finding its own voice.

Pisco is a sweet spirit distilled from grapes, whose origin is hotly contested between the neighbouring countries of Chile and Peru. If brandy is the red wine of the spirits world, then consider pisco the white.

The growth of South American wines has overshadowed pisco, which was developed in the sixteenth century when Spanish settlers arrived to set up vineyards and were looking for an alternative to their homemade "pomace" brandy – that is, made from the seemingly useless leftovers of the wine harvest.

As the popularity of this sweet spirit grew, both the Peruvian and Chilean people claimed ownership over it and now there are strictly controlled areas for pisco production in both countries, with Chilean pisco often being bottled at a lower ABV (sometimes 30%) than its Peruvian rival. However, only Peru can boast a town of the same name as the spirit, giving the Peruvians an additional claim over rights to the origin of pisco and the sole use of the term as an appellation on their labels.

Helped by a new wave of easy-to-drink blends, the appetite for this South American brandy is growing globally ... and growing fast. Currently, the biggest importer of pisco is the USA.

PISCO FLAVOURS

As with wines, the grape variety is hugely important when it comes to the style and flavour of different piscos and, again like wine, these grapes can be blended together (known as pisco *acholado*) to give each brand its own unique profile.

The most popular varieties of grapes to use are Muscat, Albilla, and Italia, the latter producing a wonderfully aromatic style of pisco, full of fragrant green apple and elderflower character, which is a great introduction to the spirit, being both sweet, unctuous, and full of fantastic aroma and flavour. Pisco *puro* brings the resonant flavours of just a single variety of grape and,

like Italian grappa (*see* p.189), highlights the true versatility of this eloquent spirit. Unlike many other fruit brandies, by law, Peruvian pisco cannot be aged in wood or anything that will lead the spirit astray from its true naked flavour profile. So no oaky overcoats here.

↓ *The Pisco Sour: one of the most moreish cocktails known to man, and very easy to make too (see p.186)!*

Meet the Maverick

» **DUGGAN McDONNELL**
SAN FRANCISCO, USA
....

Such is the demand for a Westernized style of pisco that a team of San Franciscan spirits enthusiasts (distiller Carlos Romero, sommelier Walter Moore, and bartender Duggan McDonnell) have produced their own brand, called Campo de Encanto.

It is an *acholado* style (*see* p.184), a blend of aromatic and non-aromatic grapes using a mix of Quebranta, Torontel, Moscatel, and Italia grape varieties, produced in Peru and then rested for a year. From the producer's base in San Fran, this new, accessibly flavoured, and ultra cool-looking example has become the poster boy for a new generation of pisco drinkers. It also seems to be winning its fair share of awards in spirits competitions and from drinks writers around the world.

How do you drink pisco?
Well, like brandy, pisco can be enjoyed neat at room temperature, and often is in both Peru and Chile. However, its real, spiritual home is in a Pisco Sour, the national drink of the two countries. Smooth, sweet, and refreshing, the Pisco Sour is so popular that Peru even has a national holiday to celebrate the drink. It is one of the most iconic drinks in South America.

*

Pisco Sour

The Pisco Sour is a simple cocktail to make using lime juice, sugar syrup, and egg white. Much like revenge, any sour is best served cold, and the Pisco Sour is especially good when chilled right down. It makes a great accompaniment to the national dish of Peru, ceviche, and in particular, "drunk scallops", – thinly sliced raw king scallops marinated in lime juice (the citric acid effectively "cooks" the seafood) with coriander and another healthy slug of pisco poured over the top. So here's our guide to making one cocktail, but it's easy to multiply the quantities to produce a larger batch – perfect to serve to your guests before dinner!

INGREDIENTS

50ml (2 measures) pisco
25ml (1 measure) freshly squeed lime juice
12.5ml (½ measure) sugar syrup
1 egg white

METHOD

Shake all the ingredients together with a handful of ice. Strain and serve over ice in an Old Fashioned glass. If you like, dash in some Angostura Bitters on the top.

GRAPPA

The Taste of La Dolce Vita

If there is one thing that will never be in doubt, it's the passion the Italians show towards their produce. You will find no exception in the matter of grappa production. Grappa is Italy's oldest spirit, tracing its roots back to the fourteenth century, and the technique of distilling pomace (the grape leftovers from winemaking) has been practised, refined, and mastered by generations of family-run distilleries.

Over the last two decades, grappa has undergone something of a revolution, from the traditional fairly crude spirit favoured by farmers to revivify them throughout the winter months to mass-produced grappa that abandoned the more artisanal touches of care and attention to the distillation process and the grapes used in favour of maintaining a consistent but relatively characterless product. Fortunately, the tide has turned back in favour of the craftsman, and the best grappas come from impassioned individuals who have revived the more traditional approach to the extent that the spirit is now highly regarded by connoisseurs all over the world.

When pressed, fermented, and refined, roughly 100kg (220lb) of grapes would create around 100 bottles of wine. But the pomace from such highly prized vines would only create three bottles of grappa, so making grappa on any scale is not a particularly easy business. Aromatic grapes such as Muscat and Gewurztraminer are popular with distillers for their wonderful fragrant fruity/ floral balance, but heavier varieties like Merlot, Amarone, and Barolo give the spirit an enhanced dark fruitiness, rich in jammy sweetness, spice, and tannic dryness.

Small-batch grappas are often distilled using steam-powered stills that are part pot still and part column still (*see* pp.20–1), with the steam gently lifting the characterful aromas and flavours of the pomace through the still, helping to preserve the individuality of the grape variety in the finished produce. The spirit eventually runs off at a very high 85% ABV, which is eventually cut back to a bottling strength with demineralized water.

STYLES OF GRAPPA

But grappa isn't simply an unaged spirit – oh no. Young grappa (or *giovane*) is often given a year to marry in tanks, which again helps those unique flavours come to the fore. And when it is aged, the Italians know how to select a dizzying array of different wood types. Oak, chestnut, cherry, almond, ash and mulberry are all popular with distillers, and the natural flavours extracted from the cask have to be used sparingly to get the balance and complexity in the very best examples. *Invecchiata* (aged) and the more distinct, complex, and super-aged grappas (the *riserva* and *stravecchia* styles) begin to resemble their richly coloured French counterpart brandies, with broad flavour profiles – and greater price tags to match!

> ↓ *The aromatic wafts of a world-class grappa work extremely well at the end of a meal, especially when paired with great Italian coffee.*

CLASSIC AND CONTEMPORARY SERVES

Grappa is classically served as a digestif with coffee, with a grappa glass being a work of art in itself, its thin stem and fluted shape delivering sensuous perfumed aromas above the spirit, especially at room temperature. However, it is a hugely versatile spirit, and bartenders are reaching for grappa as a fresh alternative to using Cognac and other aged brandies in classic cocktails, as well as relying on the clean, grape-driven flavour of younger, slightly chilled grappas to pep up a glass of Prosecco.

How would you describe the art of making a great grappa?
"Distilling can be a true passion! The search concentrates on the raw materials, the distillation techniques, the system knowledge, and the right interpretation of the raw materials."

How important is age versus character in grappa?
"There are two types of grappa: 'white' and aged. For the aged one, the quality of the barrels, and the time that the grappa rests is very important. 'White' grappa has to rest for two to three years in containers in order to let the distillate 'esterificate' before reducing the ABV with locally sourced water ready for bottling."

If you had one minute to tell someone why your grappa was the best, what would you say?
"We produce only pure distillates, not liqueurs or infusions, and we distil our pomace with a double distillation system, which takes at least 10 times more energy and time compared to other grappas. In addition, our grappa does not contain any additives - so it is authentic, fresh, and digestible."

What's the best way to enjoy one of your grappas?
"A 'white' aromatic grappa as an apéritif or with Stilton cheese, one made from red grapes after the coffee, and an aged grappa with a good chocolate or a Cuban cigar."

Describe Capovilla in 3 words.
"Idealist, anarchist, perfectionist."

Meet the Maverick

» **VITTORIO CAPOVILLA**
GRAPPA MAESTRO, VICENZA, ITALY

The name "Capovilla" will forever resonate throughout the world of grappa production like no other. Vittorio Capovilla is, quite simply, the father of modern grappa production and a true pioneer when it comes to creating a world-class spirit capable of carrying its unique flavours to new destinations (*see* p.197).

APRICOT BRANDY

WED.G.OUDE & C.PURMEREND

VERKOOPKANTOOR SOERABAIA

FRUIT BRANDY

Rich Regional Pickings

From Germany to South Africa, fruit brandies symbolize the wealth of variety within distilled spirits and offer a distinct insight into how distillers can bring out the key characteristics from a particular fruit. For instance, one of Germany's most popular fruit-based spirits is *Kirschwasser* or Kirsch, distilled from fermented morello cherry pulp. As freshly harvested ripened cherries are full of juice and high in sugar, they give the distiller an excellent base from which to work, but the results are perhaps not the sweet cherry flavours one would expect. Kirsch has a very clean, almost tart, intense fruitiness to it, with the underlying cherry note coming through alongside a distinct almond-like nuttiness that comes from the fermentation process, as every bit of the cherries (including the stones) are used.

EASTERN EUROPE'S TRADITIONAL TIPPLE

Across Eastern Europe, the thirst for fruit-derived brandies is remarkable, and slivovitz is a hugely popular damson plum-based brandy that is produced by fermenting the pulp and stones with yeast and then distilling in small pot stills (*see* p.20). Similarly, head to Bulgaria and you are likely to encounter a similar brandy, traditionally distilled by the Troyan monks, using locally grown blue plums and occasionally flavoured with herbs. Such is the popularity of this sweet (but powerful) spirit that the Bulgarians have dedicated an entire festival to the blue plum, with the brandy taking centre stage in the festivities and numerous home producers bringing out their stills as part of a spirited show-and-tell.

SOMERSET'S CIDER BRANDY REVOLUTION

Across the Channel from Normandy and the Calvados-producing region of France, Britain has a rich heritage of producing exceptional ciders in the southwest, especially in the county of Somerset. Here, the orchards are laden with hundreds of different varieties of apples, and the practice of converting cider into brandy is known to have existed up to the latter part of the seventeenth century, when the tradition all but died out. But two men have doggedly fought to revive the past, reclaiming Somerset's luscious orchards and once again creating an excellent spirit from the apples grown in them.

← *The skills to produce spirits are often handed down from generation to generation, remaining closely guarded within families.*
↗ *Barrels at Somerset Cider Brandy Distillery, UK. Famous for its apples, and now its casks of maturing cider brandy too.*

10

WORLD BRANDIES & EAUX-DE-VIE TO TRY

Here you will find a huge range of diversity when it comes to the flavour profiles we have chosen. As always, it's difficult to narrow such a wide-reaching spirit to just 10 exceptional examples, but the following represent some real classics.

» SOMERSET CIDER BRANDY 20 YEARS OLD
42% | Somerset, England

Purveyors of the first cider brandy in the UK since 1678, Julian Temperley and Tim Stoddart have created a flavoursome masterpiece with this, their oldest expression of brandy. The duo blends a staggering array of different apples to obtain the recipe and then the brandy is matured in oak, with just one cask bottled per year. Intense fruit leads to a very subtle, spiced note, an abundance of vanilla, and an oaky dryness.

» VIÑAS DE ORO ITALIA PISCO
41% | Peru

One of the first piscos we tried, changing our perception of this marvellous yet sometimes maligned spirit. Whereas some piscos offer harsh flavours and powerful fermented grape notes, De Oro Italia (so named after the Italia grape variety) is wonderfully floral, with a huge elderflower note alongside crisp green apple, a hint of vanilla, and ripe plums. Try this over ice, with tonic and a slice of apple. #SummerInAGlass

» VAN RYN'S DISTILLERS RESERVE BRANDY AGED 12 YEARS
38% | Stellenbosch, South Africa

With the wealth of great winemaking in South Africa, it's no surprise that category-defining brandies have begun to emerge, and Van Ryn's sits at the top of that list. Blending Chenin Blanc and Colombard, the brandy is distilled in a copper pot still and then matured for 12 years, where it develops distinct fresh-fruit notes on the nose, backed with a dark, rich spiciness and subtle earthiness on the palate.

» KORBEL CALFORNIA BRANDY AGED 12 YEARS
40% | Sonoma County, California, USA

Another place with an abundance of winemaking heritage turns its hand to making brandy – with striking success! The Korbel winery dates to the late nineteenth century, when its founder, Francis Korbel, changed direction and began making brandy. Today, it produces a range of brandies. This 12-year-old is surprisingly rich, with underlying orange zest, vanilla, and a fresh, grapey note.

» GONZÁLEZ BYASS LEPANTO SOLERA GRAN RESERVA PEDRO XIMÉNEZ BRANDY
40% | Jerez, Spain

The term "solera" is used in relation to the ageing of sherry, where older and younger sherries are blended in a wooden vat before being bottled. The same principle applies to this brandy: after 12 years, it is transferred for a final three years of maturation into rich and spicy Pedro Ximénez sherry casks, where it takes on an almost heavenly complexity, with woody spice, tobacco, and intense dried fruit.

» WAQAR PISCO
40% | Chile

There's rivalry between Chile and Peru concerning the birthplace of pisco and both countries are keen to promote their very best examples for the expanding overseas market. This one, from Camposano, a family of distillers based near Monte Patria in the region of Coquimbo, exhibits all the bold fruit and sweetness (notes of strawberry, hints of citrus zest, and honey) you would expect from the Muscat grape from which it is distilled, alongside a lingering spiciness.

» NARDINI GRAPPA RISERVA
50% | Italy

The Nardini family has been making the finest examples of Italy's national spirit since 1779. Riserva is a hugely interesting expression for those who are familiar with oak-aged spirits, as it is matured in Slavonian oak casks, produced from trees grown in eastern Croatia. The five years it has spent snoozing give the spirit an array of fruit aromas: crisp green apple, fresh lemon zest, and a perfumed nectarine note, with a honey-influenced spicy palate.

» CAPOVILLA GRAPPA DI BAROLO
41% | Italy

The undisputed master of grappa, Vittorio Capovilla truly understands the subtle nuances of a fine, artisanal spirit (see p.191). The quality of the grape harvest, the intricacies of his stills, and everything down to the hand-labelled bottles has a mark of a master craftsman about it. This expression, made using the Barolo grape variety, is very plummy and rich, with a subtle cherry note coupled with some tannic dryness and notes of cinnamon on the finish.

» LUBBERHUIZEN & RAAFF PEER CONFERENCE
42% | Netherlands

This wonderful craft distillery is built in an old fire station, but you will find nothing fiery about the spirits it produces. Everything from apples, blackcurrants, plums, cherries, and pears are turned into eau-de-vie that is aged for around a year before being bottled. This pear distillate is exactly as you would imagine: wafts of floral green fruit and an earthy bite on the palate, with more distinct soft pear and vanilla lingering.

» OKANAGAN SPIRITS CANADOS
40% | Canada

We have a friend in a Canadian band to thank for introducing us to this marvellous play-on-words of a spirit. Canados is of course an apple brandy, loosely based on Calvados. Produced by master distiller Frank Deiter at his craft distillery in Okanagan, British Columbia, Canados is full of bold, vibrant, tart fruit (using crab apples at the heart of its recipe), leaving a lingering crispness in the mouth. Anything but a pastiche, that's for sure.

OTHER
SPIRITS

The Weird, Wonderful, and Quaffable

So far our travels have taken us on an inspiring journey across the world of spirits, uncovering some outstanding expressions and delving into the passion behind producers of a wide variety of these liquors. But there are some spirits out there which, to many drinkers, are simply completely off the map: unknown or impenetrable. This chapter aims to uncover the really unusual, individual ones, especially focusing on Southeast Asia, which incredibly has some of the bestselling spirits of all time... that you've never even heard of.

AQUAVIT

The Nordic Noggin of Choice

It is a commonly known fact that both aroma and flavour are linked to memory. If this isn't something you have experienced in the past, we would recommend that you try writing some tasting notes, a task we tackle on a daily basis, and see what you come up with. Performing this exercise can be like a journey into your subconscious. As an aroma rises from a glass, it will often trigger a particular memory linked to that aroma, with the memory providing the associated tasting note.

MAY THE NORSE BE WITH YOU

One specific tasting note, for example, that we love to use is "*Star Wars* figures". It's a heady mix of plastic, paint, glue, cardboard, and print that can only be summed up in the moment when you open the package of a classic *Star Wars* figure and these aromas fill the air. There are certain aged spirits, mostly bourbon, rum, and Scotch, that occasionally give off this most evocative of aromas (in our heads anyway), taking us right back to our youths, when something as simple as a space-age plastic figure of a mythical creature could provide so much joy.

For one of us spirits explorers (Joel), an aroma that brings back so many memories of family Christmas is aquavit. Norway, either recreated at home in England or actually visited on alternate years, has played a large part in the festive celebrations in the Harrison family, with the Norwegian national spirit of *akevitt* or *akvavit*, or aquavit, as it more commonly known, holding a special place when it comes to awakening certain childhood memories.

> → *May the Norse be with you: a bottle of aquavit.*

A BIT OF HISTORY

It is said that the father of modern aquavit was Christopher Blix Hammer, a rather portly chap and a Norwegian civil servant who also served as a botanist at the University of Copenhagen during the 1700s. An extensive collector of literature, Hammer was known to write cookbooks and publish advice for farmers, which included instructions on how to distil correctly and flavour their spirits with herbs and spices harvested from their land. As a result, clear spirits with herb and spice flavours were often produced in the first instance as medicinal remedies for all sorts of aliments, and later as digestifs.

HOW IT'S MADE

Production methods are similar to that of any grain spirit, with some aquavit spirit produced in copper pot stills, while others use the more efficient column still method of distillation (*see* pp.20–1). Many aquavits that are made today are additionally matured in oak casks to add flavour and round off the harshness of the spirit.

WHAT DOES IT TASTE LIKE?

Aquavit, as we shall spell it from here on in, has a very distinct flavour and aroma. Distilled from either grain (wheat or rye) or potatoes, it is flavoured with herbs and spices from the local area, wherever in Scandinavia that may be. As with gin, each recipe is a closely guarded secret held by the distiller, with some subtle national variation between Denmark, Norway, and Sweden, but always with caraway as the main flavour (as with juniper in gin), together with a mix of other herbs and spices, including cardamom, cumin, star anise, coriander, fennel, and dill.

In Scandinavia, it is traditional to chill aquavit in the freezer and consume it as a digestif with seafood or heavy meats, such as salted sheep's ribs, often alongside a cold beer. However, there is a growing movement to sample aquavit, especially those matured for longer, such as Gilde Non Plus Ultra, which is matured for over 12 years in old sherry casks, in a way more akin to Cognac or a good whisky.

BAIJIU

The Toast of China – Gambei!

The one area of the world that we haven't yet covered is the emerging market of China.

As a business case study for spirits, China is fascinating. Previously closed to many foreign imports, the advent of the availability of good-quality Scotch, Cognac, and other dark spirits in China has seen a boom time for many of the big producers and distributors of these products, who have successfully established a platform for their spirits as super-premium products, offering high profit margins in a country with huge market potential.

Indeed, we were recently speaking to a representative from one high-end spirits company who told us that if demand for their product in China was to rise by more than three per cent in the next two years, there would be none left for their traditional Western market, and certainly none left for their home market. A major reason why sharp rises have been seen in markets such as the UK and France in, for example, the price of single malt Scotch whisky, has been Chinese demand.

But China does have its own home-grown spirit, baijiu, made from a variety of grains such as wheat, barley, sorghum, and sometimes rice and beans. These are fermented either in chambers under the ground, in clay pots.

HOW IT'S MADE

Baijiu is often distilled in column stills (*see* p.21), but a number of producers use traditional wood-lined, steam-fired Chinese stills. The spirit is then aged in clay jars, which, like a wooden cask, are porous enough to allow the spirit to breath and mellow. This also allows for baijiu producers to offer age ranges in their products, keeping them in line with much sought-after imported spirits, and fuelling a

↑ The savoury-tasting baijiu is a popular accompaniment to food in China.

secondary market for rare and collectable vintages.

Baijiu can be classed into five key classifications: strong, mild, soy sauce (a style that involves extra-long fermentation), rice, and compound (a mix of flavours favoured in baijius produced in the north of China), with one of the most highly regarded brands, Moutai, carrying powerful and sweet, soy-sauce-like aromas.

Such is the rising demand for baijiu that Louis Vuitton Moët Hennessy (LVMH), owner of Moët Champagne and premium single malt Scotch whiskies such as Glenmorangie and Ardbeg,

have taken a majority stake in a brand called Wenjun. Following in its footsteps is the world's leading drinks company, Diageo, owner of Johnnie Walker and Smirnoff, which now has a 51 per cent stake in Quanxing, another leading brand of baijiu.

WHAT DOES IT TASTE LIKE?

Baijiu has to be experienced to be understood. The flavours are herbal, slightly fruity, and at times medicinal, coupled with a heavily fermented fruit-and-hay note. There is also a distinct soy sauce note, giving it an unusual savoury flavour. It is not the most accessible of spirits to the Western palate, but it appeals strongly to the Chinese consumer.

SHŌCHŪ

Japan's National Spirit

No, NOT the better-known sake, shōchū is hugely popular in its native country, but unlike the international praise being heaped on whisky from the region, this white spirit hasn't really managed to extend its footprint beyond the four main islands of Japan.

HOW IT'S MADE

Often distilled from barley, rice, buckwheat, or potatoes, it comes in two main forms: multiple-distilled and single-distilled. The first of these is the most commercial and easily consumed, as it must be made from a mixed base of fruits or grains, distilled, and sold at less than 36% ABV.

The second variety is much more where we would expect a spirit to sit, as it must be bottled at or below 45% ABV and passed through a pot still for distillation (*see* p.20). It can then be matured but is often bottled unaged and neat, and consumed the same way.

> ↑ *Shōchū comes in a dizzying array of styles, each with its own unique flavour profile – ideal for food pairing.*

WHAT DOES IT TASTE LIKE?

As much as the producers of shōchū will be keen to tell you that their product is NOT sake (it now outsells sake in Japan), it does have some similar flavour profiles, giving off a sweet palate of dried flowers, with some seaweedy coastal notes, and a fermented orchard-fruit note to follow. A nice enough spirit that would be easy to drink once the consumer is immersed in the culture.

SOJU

The World's Most Popular Spirit

And no, we haven't been drinking... Throughout this book, we have made some pretty outlandish claims about the world of spirits, and the above subtitle perhaps tops the lot. But we can guarantee you that what we have just stated is 100 per cent true. Yes, soju, a Korean-produced spirit, is actually the most widely consumed spirit in the world. Unbelievably, according to a recent report conducted by top industry publication *Drinks International*, Jinro, the most popular brand of soju, sold 65 million cases in 2012, putting it head, shoulders, knees, and toes ahead of its nearest competitors. What that actually equates to is over half a BILLION litres (over a hundred million gallons) of spirit. That's an awful lot of exotic Martinis, is it not?

But there is no real reason why you would have had a chance to try soju unless you live in South Korea, or at least have paid a visit, as the majority of the spirit is enjoyed domestically, with only a tiny trickle making its way out of the country. However, because of its relatively low ABV – a particular style of "diluted" soju is bottled at around 20–25% ABV – it cunningly avoids the high duty prices levied on spirits in the USA, and soju is fast becoming a spirited tourist in the States, enjoyed over ice and pairing well with tonic and cola or sold in ready-to-drink cans with a mixer. In Korea, it is also a popular chaser with a beer, giving an additional level of potency to your brew.

HOW IT'S MADE

The majority of sojus produced today are colourless and unaged, distilled using rice as the base ingredient. But in the past, cheaper alternative distillates were used, including potatoes and tapioca, when the Korean population faced the unthinkable – a national shortage of rice.

↓ Like neutral-flavoured vodka, soju is easy to mix and can form the base of myriad different serves, but it is also chilled and drunk straight up.

WHAT DOES IT TASTE LIKE?

It has a similar flavour profile to a weak vodka – that is, not very flavoursome at all – with hints of prickly alcohol on the tongue, plus perhaps a lightly fermented white wine note coating the palate as it dries. But the ease with which soju can be used to add spice to fresh juice, or for that matter any soft drink, has made its appeal almost irresistible to a younger audience, who tend to be more interested in the destination of their drink rather than the ride itself.

FENI

The Goan Spiritual Experience

Spiritual enlightenment may come in many ways, but in Goa it most definitely goes hand in hand with feni – the most popular drink in this small coastal region to the west of India. Feni, or fenny as it's sometimes spelled, has captivated visitors to Goa primarily because the spirit is so scarce outside of the region. Yet around 6,000 distilleries are known to exist, producing different variations and quantities of the spirit.

→ *Feni is mainly produced from the cashew apple and is enormously popular in Goa.*

HOW IT'S MADE

Feni is derived by fermenting and distilling the juice from the cashew apple (not to be confused with the smaller, significantly harder cashew nut), and due to its unique flavours, the Goan distillers have successfully sought to have the spirit protected by Regional Indication, in the same way that Tequila or Somerset Cider Brandy (*see* p.194) have become recognized as specific national spirits. Because of the highly rustic nature of most feni producers, the techniques used in making the spirit have remained unchanged, and involve the ripened cashew apples being broken down by trampling underfoot and the pulp then pressed with a heavy weight to extract the sweet juice. It is naturally fermented for up to three or four days before being transferred to copper pot stills, where it is triple-distilled to a strength of around 45% ABV.

The north of Goa can claim as many as 4,000 tiny distilleries that produce cashew feni, but at least another 2,000 produce a different variant that is made using the sap collected from the coconut palm, which grows freely up and down the Goan coastline. The landscape of the spirit has begun to change recently, with larger brands aiming to premiumize feni in the same way that Tequila and mezcal have become more sought after by connoisseurs.

The difficulty lies in the limited availability of feni outside Goa, as the spirit is still classified as a "country liquor", which means its sale is prohibited elsewhere in India except for in a few cities up and down the west coast, with only one or two brands ever making it as far as retailers in the West.

WHAT DOES IT TASTE LIKE?

Feni is quite sweet, and despite having a slightly thin, spirity undertone has a powerful crisp, almost freshly cut green apple note alongside a distinct nuttiness that will take some getting used to if you are trying the spirit for the first time. If you can find a bottle (we recommend booking a holiday to Goa for "research purposes"), just be careful of some of the less-than-official bottlings, which may contain unpleasant-tasting surprises and dubious additives. In our opinion, it works far better as the core ingredient of a long drink over ice, as a flavouring for other drinks, or mixed with other spirits and juice in a cocktail.

5

UNUSUAL SPIRITS TO TRY

Distillation is without borders, agnostic to the idea of a true home, producing eaux-de-vie *sans frontières*, if you will.

The distilling process has been adopted and adapted by many nations around the world and here we look at some of the more unusual flavours to be found across the globe, from the Nordic countries to South Korea. The world of spirits is just that: truly global.

» LYSHOLM LINIE AQUAVIT
41.5% | Norway

....

In Norway, cask-maturing aquavit is said to date back to 1805 and a trading trip to the West Indies. Casks containing aquavit, which came home with the ship in 1807, were opened by their owners on their return to reveal the positive impact of on-board maturation. Inspired by this rich, matured aquavit, Jorgen B. Lysholm built his first distillery in 1821 and decided to release an expression, Lysholm Linie Aquavit, that would be deliberately shipped to South America and back to aid the maturation.

Today, Linie Aquavit is made from a potato-based spirit flavoured with caraway, dill, aniseed, fennel, and coriander. The spirit is filled into ex-oloroso sherry casks, adding sweet hints of vanilla. These casks are then stored on deck, shipped twice across the equator, and at sea for four-and-a-half months, subject to temperature changes, humidity, and the elements. The movement of the ship on the sea aids the maturation. At any one point, it is said that more than a thousand such casks are on a ship maturing at sea.

» JINRO SOJU 25
25% | South Korea

The world's bestselling spirit brand may be a snarling tiger in the sales department, but on the palate it's a purring kitten, with its relatively low ABV giving very little in the way of a taste-bud experience. Neat, it has a crisp freshness, with a slightly fermented grain note and a very dry finish. Probably not one for the dark spirits aficionados out there, that's for sure. But put this into context and you can make a cracking ice-cold long drink with a little soda water, some fresh lime or cordial, and a nice hot summer's day.

» SHUI JING FANG WELLBAY BAIJIU
52% | China

Listed in the *Guinness World Records* book as the oldest distillery in the world, Shui Jing Fang is over 600 years old. In 1998, an archaeological dig unearthed drying halls, fermentation pits, furnaces, wooden pillars, and the base of stills, found to be completely preserved. This spirit is well worth a try to see what distilled spirit might have been like before the idea was passed around to the rest of the world and we ended up with gin, whisky, brandy, and other flavoursome tipples.

It comes housed in a bottle with a hexagonal glass base, depicting six historic sites of Chengdu, the location of the distillery.

» KAZKAR FENI
40% | Goa, India

This might prove extremely tricky to find, as there are very few retailers outside of Goa who actually import feni – we managed to snaffle a glass or two over a superb Goan meal of Chini Raan, a delicious slow-roasted lamb shank, at a restaurant in London. So the next best option is probably to get on a plane and try it for yourself. When you do so, be prepared. Although this brand is perhaps not the most rustic of fenis you will encounter, neat it has a very powerful top note of fermented apple, crushed hazelnuts, and a spirity undertone. Its underlying future outside of Goa probably rests on using it in a mixed drink: try it as the base ingredient in a Mojito; using a touch of apple juice alongside the sparkling water, and the potential begins to emerge.

» IICHIKO FRASCO SHŌCHŪ
30% | Japan

Distilled from barley alone, this is a premium shōchū with all the hallmarks of a great production process, which leads to fantastic flavours. Distilled just once but, in a rather Japanese manner, under both low and high pressure, a spirit of around 45% ABV is achieved. This is then diluted with natural spring water to give a shōchū of incredible smoothness and consistency that has won awards the world over, as well as garnering a huge fan base of passionate drinkers in Japan.

COCKTAIL BITTERS

Seasoning of the Spirits World

Behind practically every bar you will find a mysterious collection of miniature bottles of varying shapes, usually with distinguished-looking labels. Some may even have vaguely scientific-looking dropper pipettes, clearly for measuring minute quantities of the potent elixirs inside. But just what exactly are they?

Cocktail bitters are practically indispensable in the world of the bartender. In fact, take away these tiny liquid gems and it would be almost nigh on impossible for a bartender to whip you up the large majority of classic cocktails that have been enjoyed for the better part of 150 years. Cocktail bitters are the bartender's equivalent of salt and pepper – they help shape, define, and highlight flavours in a drink, binding together the distinct balance between spirit, sweetness, and spice.

THE STORY OF BITTERS

In each of these tiny bottles lies a truly monstrous heart, full of intense flavour and aromatic power. Most bitters on the market today are modern versions of centuries-old recipes. Bitters are a blend of aromatic herbs, spices, roots, and barks that is macerated in high-strength spirit to draw out the flavoursome properties of the botanicals.

Angostura Bitters, arguably the world's most popular brand, with its distinctive ill-fitting label (supposedly a printing mistake that was retained to preserve its heritage), was a recipe developed back around 1830 as a cure-all tonic for the Venezuelan army. Infusing bitter herbs, barks, spices, and other ingredients that were believed to offer a remedy against common ailments, bitters were consumed as part of a tincture with water – for many doctors, they were the olden-day equivalent of the flu jab.

RISE, FALL, AND RESURRECTION

Bitters grew in popularity across the nineteenth century and hundreds of brands developed reputations as health tonics and restorative preparations, particularly across the USA. But the spurious claims that they could cure ailments were hard to prove, and in 1906, the Pure Food and Drug Act brought an end to the "snake oil" salesman-style pitch that most bitters companies

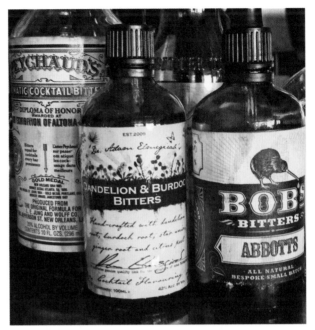

↑ *They might be small, but bottles of bitters pack an explosive and punchy aromatic flavour.*

were trading on. Seemingly overnight, confidence in bitters crumbled and only brands such as Angostura survived, giving them a competitive advantage that has remained up until today.

Until the 1990s, bitters were the unloved, misunderstood ingredient in a cocktail, but thanks to a few pioneering bartenders with a love of rediscovering the flavours of the past, old recipes (minus some of the more dubious ingredients

that probably did more harm than good) were beginning to return to the back bar.

Cocktail bitters have recently seen a huge renaissance. Bartenders are using single-varietal bitters such as clove, cinnamon, cherry, bitter wormwood, cardamom, and aniseed to enhance certain aspects of a drink, seasoning them with just a few drops of specific flavours. For want of a better analogy, you could say it is the *Pimp My Ride* equivalent of the cocktail world, with specific drinks being tailor-made using these little bottles of intense flavour. Yes, they may be small, but a little goes a VERY long way.

How to Make Your Own Bitters

Truth be told, most modern bitters recipes are superb, with each one adding a unique element of spice or herbaceousness on top of an underlying drying bitterness. But it's not as complicated as you think to have a go at making your very own bitters. Just give yourself enough time, think creatively, and have an overall picture of the sort of flavours you want to work with.

1.

KNOW YOUR BOTANICALS

As innocent as they look, some natural herbs and spices can actually produce toxins when handled improperly. First thing is to pay a visit to herbsociety.org.uk, or, in the USA, the American Botanical Council at herbalgram.org, which has a comprehensive list of things to avoid and safety guidelines. No point in poisoning yourself before you even get to have a drink. If in doubt, leave it out. Berries such as the ones from the yew tree are highly toxic.

In almost every bitters recipe, you will find a bittering agent (usually gentian, angelica, or wormwood. On their own they taste nothing short of disgusting, but when linked with other flavours they provide an important base on which to build.

2.

CREATING YOUR BOTANICAL MIX

Grab yourself as many clean jars as possible and weigh out approximately 5g (⅛oz) of each dry botanical. As a good starting guide, try to think as broadly as possible. Our recommended list of botanicals (see box, above right) will give you a great range of flavours to play with, but try going through your kitchen cupboards to see what you have in store already and for inspiration.

BEST BITTERS BOTANICALS

Gentian or angelica root
Intense bitterness

Green cardamom pods
Wonderful aromatic notes and
a hint of menthol

Star anise Dry aniseed flavours

Cinnamon bark
Rich woody/earthy notes

Clove Spicy, hot, and earthy

Dried lemon peel
Intense citrus zest

Black peppercorns Bringing heat
and a darker spiciness

Vanilla pod Buttery caramel
notes and a hint of bitterness

Dried fruit (raisins + dates)
Rich sweetness with a real depth

Coffee Earthy tones and a
toasted note

Coriander seeds A warming yet
aromatic spicy note

✷ For a very unusual note,
try **Lapsang Souchong tea**,
which will deliver a very distinct
tannic smokiness.

3.

MAKING THE INFUSIONS
....

The best extraction spirit is high-strength vodka,
which won't colour the flavour of the botanical.
Approximately 100ml (3½fl oz) per 5g (⅛oz) of
botanical will do the trick. Cover the individual
botanicals with the vodka and wait. The higher
the strength, the better refinement you will get
in your extraction. Some botanicals will start to
infuse very quickly, while others will take longer.
A rule of thumb is to check them regularly and
after two weeks you will probably get the results
you are looking for. Lighter botanicals tend to give
up their flavour more quickly, whereas the harder,
woody ones can take longer.

Experiment with higher-strength rums and
whiskies too for additional flavours in your bitters.
Overproof dark rum is superb when used to
macerate vanilla and cinnamon.

4.

BUILDING YOUR BITTERS RECIPE
....

Now comes the fun part. Filter your infusions
using coffee papers, then begin to plan how they
work together individually. Start with a foundation
of bitterness (from the angelica or gentian), next
add earthiness (cinnamon), and then start to
colour your bitters with the other flavours. Don't
forget that a little will go a long way. Cardamom is
a very dominating flavour, so watch out especially
for this little green meanie.

Aim to build up a recipe with about 50ml (2fl oz)
of liquid. Grab yourself some small bottles with
either pipette tips or plastic stoppers that allow only
a small dash to be released. Most aromatherapy
stores sell these or will point you in the right
direction. For a striking way to show off your
new bitters, urbanbar.com sells miniature bitters
decanters. They are expensive but achingly cool.

DISTILLED

—

Hop Bitters

When we discovered a cache of wild hops growing locally, we realized that we had to have a go at making some hop bitters, adapted from a recipe we found in an old medical journal from the 1870s. As hops are naturally bitter, they provide an excellent base for cocktail bitters, but also have a unique floral note that works beautifully with gin.

To make a 50ml (2fl oz) bottle, you will need the following botanical infusions. This recipe should give you a distinct balance between the bitterness of the hops, the woody notes of the cassia bark, the heat and spice of the cloves, and the medicinal/menthol note of the cardamom, coupled with a zesty backbone.

INGREDIENTS

5g (1 teaspoon) cassia bark

✳

10g (2 teaspoons) dried lemon peel

✳

10g (2 teaspoons) dried orange peel

✳

5g (1 teaspoon) cardamom

✳

5g (1 teaspoon) cloves

✳

15g (1 tablespoon) fresh hops

ANYONE FOR A TEATIME MARTINI?

Try washing out a Martini glass with a few dashes of our hop bitters before blending 50ml (2fl oz) gin with 5ml (1 teaspoon) Earl Grey-infused sugar syrup over ice in a cocktail mixing glass. *Et voilà!*

THE

21

Words Distillers Can't Live Without

Wherever they may be and whatever they may be producing, each and every distiller has a lexicon of key words that they abide by to ensure everything works. These are just 21 of the most essential...

ABV

Alcohol By Volume. The measure of alcohol as a percentage of the overall contents in a bottle.

ALCOHOL

Pretty straightforward, this one. Without alcohol, the world would be quite a dull place, wouldn't it? But to be serious for a second, every spirit contains several different kinds of alcohol, including ETHANOL (the good), METHANOL (the bad), and FUSEL oils (the ugly). The distiller's main job is to maximize the amount of good alcohols within their distillate (removing all but traces of methanol and fusel oils), backdropping the specific flavour profile of what they are creating.

CONDENSER

A vital piece of equipment that turns hot spirit vapour back into a liquid after it has been distilled. Usually seen partnered by a STILL.

CONSISTENCY

A term that can be taken two ways: most distillers try to attain a consistent flavour profile in their bottlings, whereas others celebrate the inconsistency in flavour that comes from small-batch releases, where the nuances change from batch to batch.

CUT POINT

The key moment when a distiller must begin to collect the desirable, flavoursome "heart" of the spirit run.

DISTILLATE

The liquid gold (which is ironically completely clear) that every distiller lives and breathes for. Comes in thousands of flavours, each one with its own spirited DNA – a personal statement from its maker.

DUTY

A necessary evil. Every spirit will be taxed to the high hilt – unless we are talking about a spirit produced by a "guerrilla distiller". Ssshhhhh...

ESTERS

The building blocks of flavour in a spirit come

from the chemical compounds that are produced during distillation. Esters provide the fruity, fragrant notes in a range of spirits – from whisk(e)y to brandy.

ETHANOL

This is the main type of alcohol in a spirit run that can safely be consumed; the core of every spirit and the hero in the story (*see also* METHANOL).

FERMENTATION

The all-important biochemical reaction where yeast begins to consume the natural sugars in the mash of grain, molasses, or wine, turning them into alcohol, which is then distilled.

FUSEL OILS

The rather unpleasant alcohols that in large concentration can be harmful to the human body. In small amounts, they are likely to give you a hangover. The distiller's art is to control the levels of these when they occur more abundantly near to the end of a spirit run (*see* CUT POINT). In the right quantities, they can actually be useful.

HEADS

In a pot still (*see* STILL) set-up, the "heads"

(or "fore-shots") are what first run from the spirit still. They contain a mixture of heavy and light compounds and the distiller separates them out from the quality "heart" of the spirit run to be redistilled.

LICENCE

Look at the label on most whisky bottles and you will see the word "Established", followed by a date. Then swap "Established" for "Got Caught". Every legal distillery needs a licence to distil – it's a sign that what's being produced isn't going to kill you (hopefully!).

METHANOL

Every story with a hero must have a villain, and distillers really don't want much of this criminal alcohol element in their spirit. In large quantities, it will make you go blind or, at its very worst, prove fatal.

PROOF

A measure of the alcohol level in a spirit. The term dates back to when distillers would "prove" the strength of their spirit by mixing it with gunpowder. The spirit would only ignite if it was at least "100 proof", currently agreed

as 57.1% ABV. In the USA, proof is confusingly measured as double the measure of alcohol by volume – that is, 100 proof = 50% ABV.

REFLUX

When a spirit is bubbling away in a STILL, heavier, less-desirable compounds have trouble making their way up the insides and so fall back down. In essence, reflux adds to the purification of a spirit.

STILL

The centrepiece of every distillery. Pot stills made from copper appear across the globe in whisk(e)y, brandy, Tequila, and numerous other spirits. Column stills – taller, more efficient pieces of equipment – allow the distiller to make much greater quantities of spirit in a shorter space of time and are widely used in the production of vodka, grain whisk(e)y, and rum.

TAILS

The last section of a spirit run (aka the "feints"), which contains heavier, undesirable compounds. This is separated by the distiller and mixed with the "HEADS" to be redistilled in an effort to extract consistently all the usable flavours from the spirit in question.

TEMPERATURE

Get this wrong and your fermentation won't happen, and your STILLS just won't work properly; ergo, reason enough for distillers to get a very good thermometer.

YEAST

Part of the "holy trinity" in the production of a spirit, alongside water and the base source of starch – malted barley/grain/molasses/grapes, and so on. A huge amount of the flavour in the finished spirit is owing to the action of the yeast.

YIELD

Something all distillers have to consider: how to maximize the amount of alcohol they can produce from the raw materials they have. By way of an example, a Tequila distiller will get just 1 litre (1¾ pints) of quality spirit from 7kg (15½lb) of blue agave – the plant used in the spirit's production. Malt whisky distillers can usually achieve at least 410 litres (31 gallons) of pure alcohol from 1 tonne of malted barley.

Index

Picture credits

All photographs by Andrew Montgomery except for the following: 1724 Tonic Water 43 above left. Alamy age fotostock 36; age fotostock/ J.D. Dallet 165, 167; age fotostock/José Enrique Molina 75; Ian Blyth 108; Bon Appetit/Susanna Blavarg 190; Bon Appetit/ Herbert Lehmann 171; Victor Paul Borg 203; Don Couch 71; Carl Court 204; dk 201; dpa picture alliance archive 95; Food Centrale Hamburg GmbH/Gauditz 188; Simon Grosset 31; Hemis/ Bertrand Rieger 130; Hemis/Jean-Daniel Sudres 113; Mary Evans Picture Library 34; John McKenna 126; NiKreative 134; Travel Pictures 107. Tate & Co. Distillery 138, 139. Capovilla Studio04 191. Cazulo Edric George Photography 208, 209. Chichibu Distillery 142, 143. Corbis Found Image Press 192; Janet Jarman 73; Floris Leeuwenberg 37; Danny Lehman 68; Hemis/Tuul 115; Kipa/ David Lefranc 129; Reuters/Mariana Bazo 182; Lisa Romerein 80; Swim Ink 2, LLC 166; Bo Zaunders 200. Corsair Distillery 18. Crystal Head Vodka 62, 63. Darroze Armagnacs 168, 169. Del Maguey 76, 77. Duggan McDonnell 185. Fever-Tree Limited 43 below left. Getty Images Eitan Abramovich/AFP 184; Mary Ann Anderson/ MCT via Getty Images 157; Lee Avison 81; John Burke 132; Yvette Cardozo 72; Nelson Ching/Bloomberg via Getty Images 198; Per Eriksson 153; Boryana Katsarova/AFP 194 left; Jeff Kauck 101; Seokyong Lee/Bloomberg via Getty Images 207; Christopher Leggett 93; Lonely Planet Images 94; Felix Man 100; Jeff J Mitchell 141; Pankaj Nangia/Bloomberg via Getty Images 136; Popperfoto 110; Balint Porneczi/Bloomberg via Getty Images 97; Chris Ratcliffe/Bloomberg via Getty Images 51; Heriberto Rodriguez/ MCT/MCT via Getty Images 79; David Sanger 22; SSPL via Getty Images 90, 92; Alasdair Thomson 44 below; Tohoku Color Agency 205; Universal Images Group 38; Angela Weiss 57. Hine Vintage Cognacs/Thomas Hine & Co. 162, 163. Mary Evans Picture Library Retrograph Collection 159. Medine Limited 120, 121. Overland Distillery 98, 99. Rex Features Julien Chatelin 154. Sacred Spirits Co. 46, 47. Shutterstock csp 70; Rob van Esch 44 above; gashgeron 54; IgorGolovniov 17; Steve Lovegrove 55. Sipsmith Independent Spirits 35, 39. Somerset Cider Brandy 194 right, 195. SuperStock Tips Images 181. Thinkstock iStock Editorial/Paul Brighton 206; iStock/Gutzemberg 96; iStock/Jaime Pharr 21, 128. Thomas Henry 42, 43 below right. Vestal Vodka 56.

Acknowledgements

Cheers,
Skål,
Sláinte,
Salut,
Kampai,
Prost,
Cin Cin,
Sei Gesund...

Joel & Neil would especially like to thank the following fellow "spirits explorers" for their time, patience and exceptional drinking abilities (in no particular order):

Vic Grier, Caroline & Lois Ridley, Sissel & Stuart Harrison, Denise Bates, Jonathan Christie, Leanne Bryan and all the team at Octopus Publishing, Andrew Montgomery, Claudia Young at Greene & Heaton, Dr Nick Morgan, Pat Roberts, Ken Grier, Ed Bates, Amanda Garnham, Ron Cooper, Marcin Miller, Olly Wehring, Ben Ellefsen, Cat Spencer and the chaps and chapesses at Master of Malt, Sukhinder Singh, Alex Huskinson, Duncan Ross and all at Speciality Drinks, Tim Forbes, Dave Broom, Patricia Parnell, Carla Sever, Gerry's Wines & Spirits, Alice Lascelles, David Nathan Maiser, David T Smith, Bill Owens, Clay Risen, Ted Dwane, Desmond Payne, Jim Long, Ryan Chetiyawardana, Will and Oskar at Casita, Dan Priseman and the NOLA team, Darin Jones, Jeremy Stephens, Jeremy Gara, Tim Ridley, Neil Edwards, Chris Papple, Rob Allanson, Bernhard Schäfer, Tor Visnes, Halvor Heuch and the team at IWSC.

Phew! Fancy a drink?

Distilled
by Joel Harrison and Neil Ridley

An Hachette UK Company
www.hachette.co.uk

First published in Great Britain in 2014 by Mitchell Beazley, an imprint of Octopus Publishing Group Ltd, Carmelite House, 50 Victoria Embankment, London EC4Y 0DZ
www.octopusbooks.co.uk
www.octopusbooksusa.com

First published in paperback in 2018

Copyright © Octopus Publishing Group Ltd 2014, 2018

Text copyright © Joel Harrison and Neil Ridley 2014, 2018

Distributed in the US by Hachette Book Group, 1290 Avenue of the Americas, 4th and 5th Floors, New York, NY 10104

Distributed in Canada by Canadian Manda Group, 664 Annette Street, Toronto, Ontario, Canada M6S 2C8

All rights reserved. No part of this work may be reproduced or utilized in any form or by any means, electronic or mechanical, including photocopying, recording, or by any information storage and retrieval system, without the prior written permission of the publishers.

The authors have asserted their moral rights.

ISBN: 978 1 78472 446 7

A CIP record for this book is available from the British Library.

Printed and bound in China

10 9 8 7 6 5 4 3 2 1

Senior Editor: Leanne Bryan
Copy Editor: Jo Richardson
Proofreader: Jamie Ambrose
Indexer: Cathy Heath
Art Director: Jonathan Christie
Special Photography: Andrew
   Montgomery
Picture Research Manager:
   Giulia Hetherington
Picture Researcher: Jen Veall
Production Controller:
   Allison Gonsalves